David Smith is a solicitor specialising in residential property, agency, and regulatory law. He is a partner at JMW Solicitors LLP in London. He is well known for his work in the residential property and agency field, especially in property licensing and consumer law and has advised local and national governments, large and small landlords and tenants and letting and estate agents across the sector. He has followed the GDPR since it was first announced and has provided training and advice on it to a wide range of property businesses.

# A Practical Guide to GDPR for Property Professionals

2nd Edition

# A Practical Guide to GDPR for Property Professionals

## 2nd Edition

David Stuart Nicholas Smith
Solicitor (England and Wales)
BSc (Econ), LLB, PhD (Wales)

Law Brief Publishing

Published 2022 by Law Brief Publishing, an imprint of Law Brief Publishing Ltd
30 The Parks
Minehead
Somerset
TA24 8BT

www.lawbriefpublishing.com

Paperback: 978-1-914608-33-9

*With love to D and A*

# PREFACE

I had little idea when I wrote the first edition of this book that I would be writing a second editions quite so soon. However, the growth in data protection law sparked by the GDPR has meant that things have moved quickly since the first edition. That edition had fairly sparse case references as there was no certainty that cases decided under the old regime would carry over to the new one. As a clear sign of the amount of change I have found myself making changes during the update process to incorporate new cases that have appeared along the way. In addition, the UK has departed from the EU since the first edition. This was very much on the cards when I wrote the first edition but the exact form of the departure was still very much in the air. In the end the withdrawal agreement and the changes it made were critical for our understanding of how the GDPR operates in the UK and alongside its EU variant. It has also prompted statements from government, with variable levels of believability, that they will adjust the GDPR or even get rid of it altogether. Hopefully these changes will not mean I need to start work on a third edition immediately!

The excitement created by the introduction of the GDPR has not abated. It has however changed its focus. Prior to introduction there were howls of protest from business about the damage it would do to them. Mainly, this has been muted as business has developed better understanding of what it required and some of the more panic-stricken claims for what was required by the GDPR have been shown to be wrong. However, the interest created in personal data by the GDPR and the time to consider matters caused by many people being at home during lockdown has led to an explosion in GDPR related requests and complaints. This has also led to a large number of small financial claims in the courts for alleged breaches of the regulations, some of which has been driven by law firms looking for a quick payout. More recently the courts have started to push back against this putting limits on the scope of such claims.

All of this has meant that my original purpose in writing this book to draw together the disparate themes and link them to concrete examples of use to the property sector remains the core purpose in this second edition. I have updated and added new material to reflect the clarifications provided by recent cases and new guidance and updated the text to explain how Brexit alters things. I have also taken the opportunity to talk about other real-world issues that readers of the first edition told me were missing.

As usual, I need to thank my wife and daughter who have allowed me the time to write this book. Their patience continues to be tested by me disappearing to review and write but additionally with my excitement and desire to tell them about a new GDPR case or piece of guidance. I must also thank readers of the first edition who very kindly pointed out areas they felt would benefit from more examples and explanation while generously not pointing out the failures on my part in not including these in the first place! Raj and Eric deserve a particular mention here. As always, any errors or failures to properly explain parts of the regulations are my own..

The law and guidance referred to is up to date as at 1 November 2021.

David Smith
November 2021

# CONTENTS

# CHAPTER ONE

# INTRODUCTION AND OVERVIEW

The GDPR or the Regulation (EU) 2016/679 of the European Parliament and of the Council on the protection of natural persons with regard to the processing of personal data and on the free movement of such data, and repealing Directive 95/46/EC (General Data Protection Regulation), to give it its full title, should be seen as part of a general drive to increase the controls applicable to individuals personal data.

While aspects of the GDPR have been met with howls of protest from business and it has been called impractical and an unreasonable control on business this is probably unfair. Some of the criticisms stem from misunderstandings and hysterical reporting of the restrictions. In fact, the GDPR should be seen as part of a historic and global movement to increase the control over the way business makes use of personal data.

The GDPR should be seen as part of a series of data protection measures which have a clear trajectory over time and develop in response to changes technology and the prevailing uses of data. This goes back to the early 1980s and the creation of Convention 108.[1]This convention was the first international agreement intended to control the flow of data between countries and is still in effect 40 years later with a programme underway to modernise it to deal with new technologies.[2] The development of data protection in Europe

[1] Convention for the Protection of Individuals with regard to Automatic Processing of Personal Data.

[2] https://www.coe.int/en/web/data-protection/convention108/modernised.

continued with the Data Protection Directive,[3] which was implemented in the UK by the Data Protection Act 1998. This enhanced personal protections while building on the work of Convention 108 around data transfers. The GDPR updated these mechanisms to deal with new technologies and to deal with the much increased level of data transfer inherent in the use of international cloud-based technology systems. As such it took the strongest elements of Convention 108 and the Directive and updated them while seeking to add a greater degree of consistency and an element of future-proofing so that further technological developments would be covered by the legislation.

The GDPR is not some form of European aberration. Its provisions are being mirrored in locations around the world. California has implemented the California Consumer Privacy Act (CCPA)[4]which has elements of the GDPR within it and will further implement the California Privacy Rights Act after a popular referendum which will tighten the regime further. California is not alone in the USA with Virginia and Washington States creating similar legislation. Elsewhere, Dubai has recently implemented data protection legislation which draws on elements of the GDPR and CCPA[5] while Singapore has implemented the Personal Data Protection Act (PDPA).[6] India is also working on similar legislation in the Personal Data Protection Bill. These are but a snapshot of the 145 countries that now have some form of data protection and privacy laws in place.[7] In summary, data protection laws are very much in vogue around the world and all of these laws have provisions that echo aspects of the

[3] Directive 95/46/EC of the European Parliament and of the Council of 24 October 1995 on the protection of individuals with regard to the processing of personal data and on the free movement of such data.

[4] https://oag.ca.gov/privacy/ccpa.

[5] Dubai International Financial Centre Data Protection Law No. 5 of 2020.

[6] https://www.pdpc.gov.sg/.

[7] PL&B International, February 2021, p.1.

GDPR.

The core aims of the GDPR are:

- to ensure that individuals have a very clear idea of what is being done with their data and by whom;
- to ensure that individuals have effective powers to exercise control over their data;
- to prevent evasion of legislation by moving data out of the jurisdiction;
- to ensure that data is processed only to the extent that is necessary and with a clear eye to the risks of that processing;
- to allow easy processing of data where that is beneficial to individuals;
- to create an enforcement regime which provides for effective penalties where the rules are breached.

The GDPR works primarily by creating a new concept of the Data Subject who is then provided with specific and detailed rights. A Data Subject can only be an individual, a natural person, and never a company or other legal entity. This is in fact a form of compromise by which the GDPR creates a new series of rights for individuals over their own Personal Data but without impinging on the existing system of property rights, intellectual and otherwise, of those organisations who have collected data and analysed it. Therefore it is still possible for companies to trade in and own data but individuals can also maintain their control over it. This compromise between property rights and Data Subject rights is imperfect but was almost inevitable given the very large and powerful organisations that now control so much of the world's data. In fact, the balance created by the GDPR is one that is being followed elsewhere and ultimately is likely to become the model for data protection everywhere in the end.

It is a particular choice that some object to. It is the aspiration of those who believe in blockchain (the technology that underlies Bitcoin and other crypto-currencies) that every individual would in fact control their own personal data fully and would sell it on a case by case basis to companies for them to use in exchange for a tiny payment (like a commission) for each such use. Currently this is not a model which has attracted regulators.

## The GDPR- An Overview in the UK

The GDPR, like all EU regulations, had direct effect within the UK, at least up until the point at which the UK left the EU on 31 January 2021. However, the GDPR did not stop at that point, rather it split into two versions. The EU continued to use the original GDPR (referred to as the EU GDPR throughout this book) while the UK is using its own, slightly altered, version of the GDPR[8] (called the UK GDPR in this book). The two versions are largely the same, at least initially, but will slowly diverge over time as decisions of the EU and UK courts differ and the UK authorities implement their own guidance.

In a written statement made on 3 February 2020 the Prime Minister indicated that the UK would look to develop its own separate policies for data protection, among other things.[9] More recently, the Minister for State for Media and Data said in an article that the UK would be looking to use its new independence from the EU to enhance its ability

[8] Created by the Data Protection, Privacy and Electronic Communications (Amendments etc) (EU Exit) Regulations 2019 (SI 2019/419).

[9] https://www.gov.uk/government/speeches/pm-speech-in-greenwich-3-february-2020.

to move data safely between different countries.[10] How much divergence actually occurs is open to doubt. The EU has agreed to allow the UK an adequacy arrangement which allows for the free flow of data between the EEA and UK but this arrangement is based on the UK maintaining a data protection regime which is closely allied to the GDPR. The EU-UK Trade Agreement states in its preamble that both sides recognised the autonomy of the other and their right to regulate a range of things for themselves, including privacy and data protection. This right was "reaffirmed" in a number of other parts of the Trade Agreement. Undoubtedly the UK government had a hand in inserting this to make clear that it had the right to do its own thing if it wanted to. However, the same preamble also states that the parties recognise the value in free flow of data while respecting data protection rules and so there is an in-built warning that excessive divergence could undermine that free flow. Therefore, in practice, UK divergence is likely to be more related to developing guidance which seeks to ensure that the GDPR operates in a light touch manner and also ensuring that it enters into trade arrangements which allow for safe data transfer to new trade partners as opposed to more radical alteration to the core parts of the UK GDPR.

The GDPR is very much a risk-based system. Processors of data are encouraged to carry out risk assessments as to their activity and the potential risks to both security and the rights of individuals. This places a heavy obligation on business to ensure that they are complying with the GDPR. This is because the GDPR operates by making general statements of what needs to be achieved but exactly how business does so is something that is for them to decide.

When looking at the UK GDPR it is important to give some consideration to its nature when reading it. Both its original nature as something which emerged from the EU as well as its altered nature as a post-Brexit EU-UK hybrid. Like all legislation which emanates from

---

[10] PL&B UK, March 2021, p.1

the European Union it needs to be considered as a whole as well as in parts. The recitals that act as an introduction and form a pre-amble to the GDPR need to be read with some care as they provide a great deal of additional information that both modify the understanding of the main articles and add a great deal of important detail. These recitals still exist in the UK GDPR and are still a key element of that interpretation. Frustratingly, they have not been modified in the same way as the main part of the UK GDPR and so parts of them no longer entirely make sense in terms of the UK GDPR as it now applies. For example, the recitals still make reference to the European Commission and these have not been altered. When considering the GDPR in a UK context such references will presumably need to be ignored. The actual provisions of the GDPR have also been modified for the UK.[11] However, these changes are not fully up to date at the time of writing in the main publicly-accessible legislative resources. Fortunately, there is a consolidated document showing all the changes in a tracked format (known as a Keeling Schedule).[12] For each section it is also necessary to consider the DPA 18 which then modifies parts of the GDPR by providing various derogations and limits on its scope of operation. Finally, because the GDPR aims at general statements it is then useful to review the appropriate guidance on the topic. Any guidance provided by the European Data Protection Board (EDPB) as well as guidance produced by its precursor body the Article 29 Working Party (Art 29 WP) which was issued prior to 31 January 2021 is applicable to the UK GDPR (obviously with edits to remove reference to EU institutions) unless it has been replaced by UK specific guidance. It is likely that the UK ICO will adopt some of these

[11] Principally by the Data Protection, Privacy and Electronic Communications (Amendments etc) (EU Exit) Regulations 2019.

[12] Keeling Schedules showing changes which would be affected by the Data Protection, Privacy and Electronic Communications (Amendments etc)(EU Exit) Regulations 2019 as amended by the Data Protection, Privacy and Electronic Communications (Amendments etc)(EU Exit) Regulations 2020. Available at: www.gov.uk/government/publications/data-protection-law-eu-exit [last accessed: 15 July 2021].

guidance documents explicitly and will also produce its own. If the guidance was produced after 31 January it is not binding in the UK and far less likely to be relevant but may still be useful as a guide to practical implementation of parts of the UK GDPR. It may also be useful to consider guidance produced by other data protection regulators in the EU in terms of practical matters. The Irish DPC often produces useful guidance relevant to the property sector, for example. The guidance of the Information Commissioner's Office (ICO) will however now be the primary source of guidance on the UK GDPR. All of this is quite an involved process and in practice most people will short-circuit this by heading straight for the guidance on the ICO's website. However, it is worth bearing in mind that the ICO's views as expressed on their website are just their views and ultimately it is the courts that will have the final say as to how the UK GDPR should be interpreted. The ICO's guidance is also quite summary and generic in nature although that is now starting to change as it takes over primary responsibility for the management of the UK GDPR. Finally, it is important to understand that the ICO guidance will be an increasingly weak guide to the operation of the EU GDPR as the UK view diverges from that of the rest of Europe and in those cases it will be necessary to consider the guidance produced by the EDPB in more detail. Naturally, my aim is to allow readers to avoid all of this by providing most of what is needed in one place!

## Ambit

The UK and EU GDPR have a purposely wide ambit. Unlike previous data protection regimes in the EU which only applied within the EU the UK or EU GDPR both apply to any Data Controller or Processor processing Personal Data inside the UK or EEA but equally to any Controller or Processor processing personal data which belongs to a citizen of the UK or EEA, regardless of where the Controller or Processor is based or where they do the processing. This extra-territorial scope, applying the GDPR to both to any person providing goods or services within the UK or EEA or monitoring the activities of UK or EEA citizens is also found in other recent privacy legislation. The California Consumer

Privacy Act also seeks to apply to any organisation doing business with citizens of California, regardless of where they are ultimately based. Naturally, there is some question over how enforceable any of these rules are in practice but the general principle that they are seeking to espouse holds good. The key point is that it is not possible to avoid the GDPR simply by moving data out of the UK or EEA. In addition, for any business that is dealing with citizens of California, as well as several other jurisdictions, they will need to comply with the data protection rules that protect those citizens as well as the relevant GDPR. Therefore, many businesses will need to comply with more than one data protection regime. In practice, for UK and EEA businesses this is not as bad as it might seem, as compliance with the relevant GDPR is likely to create compliance with most other similar regimes.

There is a degree of subtlety in all this but it is a question which is increasingly important as the UK and EU separate and each have their own flavour of the GDPR. Which one does a business need to comply with? The High Court has actually considered this question in relation to the application of the EU GDPR before the UK fully separated but the principles are applicable to both situations.[13]

The key points to bear in mind are:

1. A Data Controller or Processor may have some of its activities subject to the relevant GDPR while others will not be.

2. To be established in a country an organisation must have a stable arrangement which seeks to provide services within that jurisdiction. A generic service that is available to all but happens to be used by persons within a specific jurisdiction without being actively targeted at them will not meet this test.

3. Just because an organisation is able to and prepared to sell goods or services in a specific country does not mean it is processing the data

[13] *Soriano v Forensic News LLC & Ors* [2021] EWHC 56.

of people in that country.

4. Even the placement of cookies or other web trackers on computers of persons in a country that access a website is not enough to engage the GDPR if those cookies are only for generic advertisement tracking as is common across the internet as a whole.

So, a company that offers letting agency services in the UK and mainly deals with UK property applicants would be subject to the UK GDPR for that work. Even if a single applicant contacted them from France that would not change as it would not be a stable arrangement.

However, if the same company specifically targeted Irish landlords, had a website actively seeking those landlords and had Irish based representatives to meet with them all in order to encourage them to invest in rental properties in Liverpool then that would be an activity that would be subject to the EU GDPR. As well as the EU version this activity would also be subject to the UK GDPR as the processing would be taking place in the UK.

The two activities outlined above might well co-exist alongside one another in the same organisation and so parts of the data being processed by that organisation would be subject solely to the UK GDPR and other subject to both UK and EU GDPR.

# CHAPTER TWO

# PERSONAL DATA AND PRINCIPLES

Classically, it was the general view of the courts and most commentators that personal data needed to identify an individual relatively closely, usually by name. The GDPR has moved away from such a narrow approach and classifies Personal Data as any data which serves to uniquely identify an individual, whether to the public at large or just to a specific Data Controller. This includes a name but can equally include an email address or even a number or other identifier applied by the Data Controller themselves. Likewise, using data which is uniquely associated with an individual such as the IMEI number which identifies their mobile telephone, the IP address which identifies their internet connection, or a cookie placed on their computer would all qualify as Personal Data. These changes reflect the much greater association of individuals with technology which is unique to them and identifies them closely. Equally, data can be Personal Data if items within it can be grouped together in order to identify people. By the same token data is still Personal Data if it can be used with other available data to identify a person. So, splitting data up within the Data Controller's systems so that individuals can only be identified if the data is grouped back together is generally ineffective as a means of avoiding the GDPR because the data taken together can still be used to identify individuals. This change reflects the very much greater data storage capabilities of organisations which allow the storage of sufficient data to easily identify people as well as the search power of the internet which will often allow identification of people by searching for distinctive characteristics rather than their names. This makes the use of pseudonymisation ineffective as a means of avoiding the GDPR. However, pseudonymisation is still a useful data management strategy as it reduces the risk of sensitive data loss and means that if data is lost or compromised it is potentially less damaging because it will be harder to link the personal data to a real person.

However, data is only Personal Data if it is about an individual operating in their personal capacity. So data about a company is not Personal Data. However, the collection and use of data about individuals within that company for business purposes (for example their name, contact details and interests for marketing purposes) is Personal Data although the GDPR would take a light touch approach to this usage. The collection of data about a sole trader or about the employees of a company for reasons which relate to them as individuals is very definitely Personal Data and this will attract more interest. So, an estate agent that collects and maintains a list of conveyancing solicitors for professional reasons associated such as referring buyers and sellers and keeping in touch with the conveyancing of properties is the collection Personal Data albeit data they can be relatively relaxed about using. However, collating the same list of conveyancers because the estate agent has a lot of high value property and is of the view that they are wealthy and likely to be interested in purchasing that type of property is now the collection of data about employees of companies but for a purpose that is personal to them. Therefore, this use of Personal Data would be much more sensitive. The data itself is unchanged but the purpose of collection is different. As always with the GDPR it is also important to remember that the collection of data for one purpose does not allow its use for another purposes. So in the example above, collecting names and email addresses of conveyancing solicitors for business use and then using them to market high value properties to those people would be unacceptable.

Data must also relate to an individual if it is to be Personal Data. This means it must actually be about them or connected to them in some way. So, a list of individual's job titles with the companies they work for could be Personal Data if those job descriptions were sufficiently specific (or the roles sufficiently unique) to allow identification of an individual. However, if the job titles were generic and could refer to a number of people then it would not be personal data as it would not relate to anyone specific. Likewise, a salary on a job advert is not Personal Data because it does not relate to a person but once someone is hired at that salary for that role the data would become Personal Data because it would then relate to them.

The GDPR talks a lot about the processing of Personal Data. However, it is important to understand that this is a very wide concept. Storage of data is also a form of processing so it is not a sufficient answer to the GDPR for a party to assert that you are not doing anything with Personal Data, merely storing it. In addition, while the GDPR, and a lot of the writing and examples that surround it, are clearly, and quite rightly, directed toward the electronic storage and processing of data the regulations are no less applicable to more traditional storage on paper. Indeed, any form of storage medium – historic, current, or future is within the reach of the GDPR and that is a key objective of the GDPR.

## The Data Protection Principles

There are seven core principles which underlie the GDPR. These are:

1. Lawfulness, fairness and transparency
2. Purpose limitation
3. Data minimisation
4. Accuracy
5. Storage limitation
6. Integrity and confidentiality (security)
7. Accountability

These show some variation from the principles established under the older data protection regime. Some of the principles that existed under the previous regime, specifically those relating to processing within the rights of the Data Subject and not transferring data outside the area have been removed as they are dealt with elsewhere in the GDPR. There is a new principle added regarding accountability and there is increased emphasis on transparency and clarity as to how and why data is being processed.

Looking at the principles in more detail they are:

- Lawfulness, fairness, and transparency- Personal Data is to be "processed lawfully, fairly and in a transparent manner". That means that Personal Data must be processed in a way that is compatible with the GDPR but more importantly in a way that provides a fair balance between the rights of the Data Subject and the Data Controller and that this balance must be fully and clearly explained to the Data Subject so that they can understand it. This is similar to the principle under the old regime but with the important addition of transparency. This emphasis on transparency is new within the GDPR and is a key component of the new regime and what it is seeking to do. A great deal of the practical day-to-day work of the GDPR relates to this principle. Contrary to popular belief the GDPR is intended to promote the use of data by business but it also focuses heavily on ensuring that the use is well understood by Data Subjects;

- Purpose limitation- Personal Data must be "collected for specified, explicit and legitimate purposes and not further processed in a manner that is incompatible with those purposes". This means that when Personal Data is collected it must be for purposes that are lawful and are set out to the Data Subject. Again, this is similar to the old regime but with the addition of the word "explicit". Again, this illustrates the changing emphasis of the GDPR and its emphasis on being very clear with Data Subject's as to how their Personal Data is to be used. This principle is important because it blocks, and is intended to block, organisations from collecting data for one declared purpose and then using it for something else;

- Data minimisation- Personal Data collection is to be "adequate, relevant and limited to what is necessary". This is largely unchanged from the old regime except that the GDPR puts a far greater emphasis on limitation and justification of the volume of data that is being collected and how long it is to be retained for. There has been criticism levelled at the property sector for excessive data collection in some cases. Minimisation has become an increasingly important aspect of the GDPR and one where violations are being called out more often. A recent case in the County Court excited press interest as it related to a popular brand of doorbell and home security camera.[14] This involved a neighbour dispute because one individual had positioned security cameras such that they overlooked the property of their neighbour. While this was claimed to be for the purpose of security the court found that security did not justify the level of intrusion the camera placement created. The use of security cameras is increasingly common and is a matter of serious concern for the GDPR. Where these are being used then either explicit consent will be needed or there will need to be a clear legitimate interest for the recording. The ICO has been clear in its guidance that such legitimate interests are very limited and are very unlikely to justify observation of other people or their property on a routine basis. Security cameras will be acceptable but care must be taken with siting so that they do not observe another person's property unnecessarily. Similar principles apply to the recording of audio, including call recording. An organisation

[14] See https://www.bbc.co.uk/news/technology-58911296

seeking to record calls will need to either have consent to do so or will need to have a clear basis for doing so. Where there is a statutory basis such as a requirement to record calls by the FCA or some other body this is unlikely to be an issue. However, other organisations will need much greater justification. The Telecommunications (Lawful Business Practice) (Interception of Communications) Regulations 2000[15] allow recording for establishing the existence of certain facts. This is commonly used as a justification where contracts are being entered into orally over the phone. It will be harder to justify recording in other circumstances;

- Accuracy- Personal Data is to be "accurate and, where necessary, kept up to date". This is self-explanatory and again similar to the previous regime. Again, however, the GDPR places a much stronger emphasis on this requiring that "every reasonable step must be taken to ensure that personal data that are inaccurate ... are erased or rectified without delay";

- Storage limitation- Personal Data is to be "kept in a form which permits identification of data subjects for no longer than is necessary". This principle is almost completely unchanged from the previous regime;

- Integrity and confidentiality- Personal Data is to be "processed in a manner that ensures appropriate security of the personal data". This is also almost completely unchanged in wording. The real change comes from the substantial changes in the IT security world in the time since the older data protection regime was commenced;

---

[15] https://www.legislation.gov.uk/uksi/2000/2699/contents/made

## Accountability

The final principle, accountability is wholly new to the GDPR. It is not a principle like the others in that it is listed separately in its own sub-section. The accountability principle requires that Data Controllers are responsible for and able to show their compliance with all the other principles. The key importance of this principle is that there is an ongoing requirement to be able to be able to demonstrate compliance with the GDPR. In other words, it is not enough to just "get lucky" with the GDPR and not have a data breach that is noticed. Data Controllers should be able to show how they comply with the GDPR to anyone who asks at any time. This does not mean that supervisory bodies, like the ICO, will be knocking on the door of Data Controllers and asking them to prove their compliance (although they could) but where a data breach occurs the ICO will not just be looking at the breach itself but rather the entire sweep of GDPR practices operated by the Data Controller to assess whether the Data Controller was generally in compliance with the GDPR. This demonstrable compliance will have a significant effect on how a supervisory body judges a Data Controller who has breached the legislation and will ultimately be the difference between a finding of a Data Controller having been in compliance but being a victim of hacking or ill-luck and a finding of lack of compliance, with penalties to suit. It should be borne in mind that the ICO, in common with most regulators, has tended to move away from an investigation-based compliance model where they interview people and actively visit companies to investigate breaches to a desk-based compliance model. This means that compliance is much more focused on the existence of proper policies and records and less on investigations into what in fact occurred in any specific breach. So making sure that paperwork is completed and up to date is of particular importance when thinking about the GDPR.

Accountability is also there to deal with a part of the GDPR that some users object to. It is deliberately relatively woolly in that it generally shies away from specific actions that Data Controllers and Data

Processors are required to take and focuses instead on outcomes that are meant to be achieved. The GDPR in many ways parallels the movement that many legal professionals will be familiar with (although again many do not much like it!) from prescriptive rules to more general statements of desired outcomes that Data Controllers should meet. This allows for a degree of latitude in data processing activity and the use of professional judgement. As against this, an approach like this creates concern among businesses that they will be penalised for things that they might view as reasonable. This flexibility is why the GDPR, and its regulators, prize impact assessments and clearly written policies which allow business to demonstrate careful consideration and justify their data usage decisions. This flexibility and focus on outcomes rather than specific tasks is also one of the ways that the GDPR is future-proofed and designed to embrace novel technologies and their use of data. It does not make prescriptive rules about what must be done but rather sets out what must be achieved. If a new technology emerges then provided it achieves those things that the GDPR seeks in respect of Personal Data, then the manner in which it gets there is of limited concern.

Actually meeting the accountability principle is a little more complex in practice! It is not a box-ticking exercise and so there is no simple answer as to what any one organisation must do. It is probably possible for many organisations to simply download a set of pre-written policies and templates and use these but doing so means that they are likely to miss out on some of benefits of the flexibility the GDPR provides. Ideally, though, organisations must actively think about data protection and be structured and proactive about how they deal with it.

**What do we need to do to be accountable?**

Accountability is not a box-ticking exercise. Being responsible for compliance with the GDPR means that you need to be proactive and organised about your approach to data protection, while demonstrating your compliance means that you must be able to evidence the steps you take to comply. It can be difficult to be concrete about what accountability means as at one level it simply means that organisations must comply with the GDPR.

In order to help with meeting the accountability principle the ICO has created an accountability framework which enables organisations to take a self-assessment and form an action plan to ensure they are complying with the GDPR. The framework enables organisations to work through ten categories building towards demonstrable compliance with the GDPR. For smaller organisations, especially, the accountability framework is a valuable tool which brings together existing ICO guidance in a useful structure that will help organisations meet the standards required. However, it does not provide policies and procedures in itself and so there is still considerable work to do.

While the GDPR does not specifically require a data protection policy it is almost impossible to comply without one. This means that at a very minimum organisations will need one or more suitable and proportionate policies on how they will handle Personal Data of the type that they are going to collect. Such policies would be expected to set out:

- A general organisational commitment to the principles of the GDPR;

- In broad terms, what Personal Data is being collected and what it is being used for. This might be done by way of a Data Protection Impact Assessment (see below);

- Who is to access the Personal Data and for what purpose;
- How the Personal Data is going to be secured;
- How and when the Personal Data is to be deleted;
- How often the policy is to be reviewed.

A larger organisation would be expected to do much more. In a larger organisation the above would probably need to be broken down into a range of policies with each of them having considerably more detail. At this level there would be an expectation of policies to cover:

- Assessment of new processes and systems for GDPR compliance. This is also known as Data Protection by Design;
- Internal audit and evaluation mechanisms;
- A process for the internal and external reporting of data breaches;
- How staff are to be trained and updated on the GDPR.

It may be necessary for a larger organisation to have more than one policy to account for different uses of different data. For example, a policy aimed at use of customer data would be quite different from a policy dealing the use of employee data. Smaller organisations are not generally expected to have policies for these additional items but they will need to have considered them and will need to have achieved the same overall outcome.

Accountability is a real issue which regulators take seriously. A German data protection regulator, the Berlin Commissioner for Data Protection and Freedom of Information, fined a company called

Deutsche Wohnen 14.5 million, largely for failing to have a compliant policy for data retention and deletion. While this case is exceptional it demonstrates the substantial importance the GDPR places on compliant policies and the very real consequences of not having them.

## Data protection by Design and Default

Part of the accountability principle is the concept of Data protection by design and default. Essentially this means ensuring that GDPR compliance is built into data processing activities from the moment they are initially envisaged and not added as an afterthought. Too often under the old regime a process would be created and substantially implemented and then, at a relatively late stage, data security and protection would be bolted on. This led to imperfect data protection compliance which often left organisations largely unable to comply with Data Subject requests.

Article 25 makes clear that the concept of protection by design means that from very first principles the GDPR need to be designed in. This means designing processes to ensure that they need the very minimum amount of Personal Data and that it is anonymised wherever possible. This also means ensuring that Personal Data is stored in such a way that it is highly secure and that even if it is stolen it is unlikely to be of use to a computer criminal. So it should be encrypted within the storage medium and ideally the data should be separated so that names and addresses which easily identify individuals are separated from other Personal Data to reduce risks if data is stolen. It also means designing data storage so that it can be easily searched to locate Personal Data and so that records can be partially or fully deleted to comply with Data Subject requests to utilise their rights under the GDPR. In practical terms it would probably mean placing fields into data records which allowed for them to be flagged as subject to erasure or restriction based on the exercise of a Data Subject's rights (see below) and then ensuring that a search of data records did not bring up entries that had been flagged in this way. Finally, it requires ensuring that the mechanisms which access Personal Data are designed in such a way that they are secure against external penetration but also secure against internal misuse so that they have proper access control implemented such that only employees who need access to Personal Data have that access and they only have access to the Personal Data they truly need.

Recital 78 makes clear that the process of design goes much further than software and also includes the design of internal policies so that staff are properly trained and understand their obligations. It also requires that where software or services are being purchased that the design principle is taken into account and purchasing decisions include assessing GDPR compliance.

This is the reason why it is not open to organisations to say that they are unable to comply with Data Subject rights such as a request for access to data because it is too complex or expensive for them to comply. If systems have been properly designed with data protection in mind, as the GDPR requires, then compliance with rights will be easy.

## Data Protection Officers

The GDPR created a new role of the Data Protection Officer or DPO. This is a person within and organisations who assists the senior leadership of an organisation by informing and advising on GDPR obligations, monitor compliance, manage the DPIA process and act as a central point of contact for Data Subjects and the relevant supervisor on all GDPR issues. DPOs are not personally responsible for GDPR compliance (although they can be at an organisational level), that remains the duty of the organisation and its directors.

Public bodies must have a DPO as must organisations that carry out large scale monitoring of individuals on a regular basis or process large amounts of special category data as a core activity. Other than these organisations, appointment of a DPO is optional.

The Law Society has produced guidance for law firms which takes the view that they are not involved in large scale data processing as a core activity. This is because recital 97 states that a core activity means the primary activity of the organisation and not processing that is carried out as an ancillary activity. As law firms are primarily engaged with legal work their data processing activity is only ancillary. A similar rationale would apply to most organisations working within the property sector. However, the Law Society also suggests that law firms should consider appointing a DPO on a voluntary basis.

A DPO can be appointed by a Data Controller or a Data Processor if one or other of them are engaged in activity that falls within the requirements of the GDPR. The fact that a Data Controller is obliged to appoint a DPO or chooses to do so does not oblige a Data Processor to appoint a DPO and vice versa. For example, a small law firm provides health insurance and occupational health services to its staff through a subcontractor who is acting as a Data Processor. This sub-contractor is providing similar services to many firms and so it heavily involved in processing health data which is special category data. Therefore the subcontractor requires a DPO. However, this need on the part of the sub-contractor does not oblige the law firm to have a DPO.

Several organisations can share a DPO. This could be either on the basis that they are group companies and so choose to share specific administrative services or it can be on the basis that a company has chosen to subcontract its DPO responsibilities.

Article 37(5) specifies that a DPO should be chosen on the basis that they have expertise in the GDPR. The level of expertise and the formality of the qualifications required of a DPO depend on the size of the organisation and the volume an sensitivity of the Personal Data it is handling. The Art 29 WP has produced guidance on DPOs which states that it is desirable for the DPO to have a good knowledge of the relevant business sector as well as knowledge of the business of the appointing organisation and its data processing activities. A DPO should also have a good understanding of data security and information technology both in a general sense and as they are used by the relevant organisation. Article 38 requires the organisation to involve the DPO in any issue relating to the protection of Personal Data. This will require a DPO to occupy a position of substantial trust in an organisation as they will need to be consulted on any new data processing operation, which may be commercially sensitive, at an early stage. When a DPIA is conducted the GDPR in Article 35(2) expressly requires that the DPO is consulted during its preparation.

An organisation is required by Article 38 to actively support their DPO by providing them with sufficient resources to carry out their tasks. Article 38 also requires that an organisation may not tell the DPO how to go about their duties and they cannot be dismissed or penalised in any way for carrying out their role. Article 38 also requires that a DPO reports to the highest level of the organisation so they will need to be on the board or close to it.

The Art 29 WP also suggests that a DPO should be provided with resources to continuously develop and improve their skills and knowledge and access to other organisational services (HR, legal etc) to allow them to be monitored as well as to allow access to those services to support the work of the DPO.

Organisations must publish details of who their DPO is and provide their contact information to enable Data Subjects and organisation staff to contact them easily. They are also obliged to inform the relevant data protection supervisor of who the DPO is.

## Impact Assessments

The GDPR favours the use of impact assessments, known as Data Protection Impact Assessments (DPIAs) as a means of demonstrably complying with the GDPR. They are also a key element of the accountability principle as they show a Data Controller explicitly considering compliance with the GDPR. Article 35 requires a Data Controller to carry out a DPIA where there is a likelihood of a high risk to the rights and freedoms of Data Subjects. The EDPB has endorsed guidance from the Art 29 WP that sets out nine categories of higher risk processing and this guidance states that any processing that engages two or more of those categories is very likely to require a DPIA. These categories are:

1. Any form of evaluation or scoring particularly where this scoring is based on work performance, economic status, health, behaviour or interests. This would include the use of credit referencing and AML database checks and so is likely to be met by most letting and estate agents and law firms.

2. Automated-decision making that has a legal or similar effect. This would include making decisions to offer or refuse a contract based on an automated decision that did not involve a person. Some of the new technology being introduced to assess contracts or offer consumer credit automatically would fall within this category.

3. Systematic monitoring by automatic means such as CCTV with facial recognition technology for example.

4. Handling of special category data or data of a sensitive or highly personal nature such as health data or financial information.

5. Large scale data processing involving large numbers of individuals or large numbers of records.

6. Any system which combines data sets from two different sources to create new information about Data Subjects.

7. The processing of data about vulnerable Data Subjects such as children or the elderly.

8. Innovative processing and the application of new technologies. This might include facial recognition technology or the embedding of technology into common consumer devices.

9. The data processing prevents a Data Subject accessing a service or modifies the service on offer. This would include a letting agent doing a tenant reference for example to decide the terms of a tenancy agreement.

This list is not exhaustive but gives an idea of the kind of considerations that would be relevant. Tellingly it also means that a lot of property related matters are likely to be high risk.

So a letting agent using a credit score and former landlords reference to decide whether to offer a tenancy and what terms to offer it on would fall within categories 1 and 9 and also potentially category 6 due to the combination of data sets. Therefore this is likely to be a high risk processing exercise which requires a DPIA. Thinking about the effect of such processing, which might decide whether a Data Subject is able to access a home and how much they have to pay for it in rent it becomes clear that this activity is likely to need a DPIA.

Likewise, a conveyancer carrying out AML checks as part of their standard KYC processes will meet category 1. If some of their clients are vulnerable such as elderly people then they will also meet category 7 and so they are also likely to need to carry out a DPIA. As conveyancers will also be handling a wide range of fairly sensitive data such as financial information they will likely meet category 4 as well.

A DPIA can be carried out on a single discrete process, such as a letting agent assessing its tenant referencing process or it can be carried out in respect of all processing. The ICO recommends that where a DPIA has not been done before, an overarching assessment is carried out on the entire data process and then discrete ones are carried out on any new process that is introduced.

It is important to understand that a DPIA is there to look at the overall process and does not deal with specific individuals. So it would not be appropriate to pick a single individual and do a DPIA from their point of view. The DPIA should be carried out on the process considering all of the Data Subjects whose Personal Data might be put through it.

## How to do a DPIA

There is no set format for a DPIA. The GDPR purposely sets out a broad framework for a DPIA only. This is to enable Data Controllers to choose the methodology that best fits with their existing working practices and to allow them to dovetail the DPIA with their current risk and audit processes. It is also intended to allow flexibility for different industries and sectors to use a DPIA methodology that best fits their particular needs and the way they operate. Notwithstanding this flexibility the GDPR sets out in Article 35(7) some elements which a DPIA must address. The Art 29 WP has taken tis into account and suggested a broad 7 step process for carrying out a DPIA. This involves:

1. Describing the data processing- The data processing that the DPIA is considering must be set out. There is no requirement to do this in writing and an ideal way to do so is by setting out a graphical data journey which shows the movement of Personal Data through systems and processes as a flowchart.

2. Assessing the necessity and proportionality of the processing- this step considers how important and necessary the processing is. For example, could it be carried out in a different way that

would use less or no Personal Data? This will also include identifying the relevant processing bases for each part of the processing and cover such operational issues as preventing creeping increase in Personal Data usage, ensuring the data is and remains accurate, ensuring the data is minimised as far as possible and meeting the various Data Subject rights.

3. Consider currently proposed measures- this stage involves considering the initial measures put in place to meet the general requirements of the GDPR. As the GDPR requires a data protection by design approach there should have been some thought given to meeting the requirements of the GDPR at the earliest stages. Where the DPIA is examining a historic processing structure that pre-dates the GDPR this step will be more focused on describing and assessing the measures that protect data security and integrity that are already in place and well they accord with GDPR standards.

4. Assess the risks to Data Subject rights and freedoms- this step is the meet of a DPIA. It requires an objective look at the process and an assessment of where it might infringe on the GDPR rights. This should particularly look at the level of control a Data Subject can exercise over the Personal Data and the level of damage that could be done to a Data Subject either through the anticipated use of the Personal Data or through its abuse. This stage would also include consulting with relevant stakeholders, especially a DPO if the organisation has one.

5. Measures to address risks- Once the risks have been assessed then measures can be put in place to mitigate them. This could include improving information provision to Data Subjects, limiting the Personal Data being collected, cutting back on the processing, anonymising data, or improving security.

6. Document- A DPIA needs to be documented and then

approved at or near board level. It should also have a specified review date.

7. Monitor and review- The purpose of carrying out a DPIA is not to allow it to gather dust. It needs to be monitored to ensure that the processing is being carried out in the manner the DPIA anticipated and then repeated if the processing operation changes. It should also be reviewed on a regular basis to make sure that it remains accurate and also to re-assess the mitigation measures to see if they can be improved.

As the Art 29 WP has said the DPIA process outlined above is iterative in nature. Both in the sense that the assessment process, especially straps 3 to 5 inclusive, will need to be cycled through several times in the preparation of the DPIA but also in the sense that once the DPIA is completed it will need to be monitored and repeated at an appropriate stage, either when things change or as part of a regular review. The ICO also has guidance on carrying out a DPIA which uses a very similar stepped process. They also produce a template to assist in preparing a DPIA.

Where a DPIA concludes that there is high risk to Data Subject rights but further concludes that this risk cannot be mitigated to any significant extent there is an obligation to report this the relevant data protection supervisor and to provide them with a copy of the DPIA.

# CHAPTER THREE
# PROCESSING

## The Processing Bases

When processing Personal Data under the GDPR it is essential to establish a lawful processing basis to do so. This must be one of the approved processing bases provided for within the GDPR. The approved processing bases are set out in Article 6 of the GDPR and are:

- Contract- processing to allow a contract to be entered into or to comply with the requirements of a contract;

- Legal obligation- processing required by the law or a court order;

- Vital interests- processing necessary to protect life;

- Public task- processing required to allow a public body to carry out an official role which they are required or authorised to do by law;

- Consent- the Data Subject has given consent for processing for a specific purpose;

- Legitimate interests- processing is necessary to protect the legitimate interests of the Data Controller or the legitimate interests of someone else.

Before discussing the processing bases in more detail it is important to note that a lawful processing basis alone is not enough. All of the processing bases, other than consent, require that the processing is necessary. Recital 39 to the GDPR makes clear that this means that the processing is limited to what is required to achieve a reasonable purpose and is the most reasonable means of achieving that purpose. So, if a purpose can be achieved without processing Personal Data or could be achieved by processing data anonymously then it would not be a legitimate use of the data. For example, a conveyancer wishes to collect statistics on sale prices of residential property for marketing purposes. To do this they send their client's names, date of birth, property address, and the final purchase price to a third party which collates this data and provides a graphical representation to the conveyancer of house price change by postcode area. However, the same data could be found by simply providing the third party with the first part of the postcode of the property and the eventual sale price as there is no need to break the data down further. The name of the client is irrelevant. Therefore, the Personal Data processing in this case is not necessary to achieve the objective and so would not meet the requirements of the GDPR. In the property sector, the Irish Data Protection Commission, has issued guidance on the collection of personal data from prospective tenants[16] and from those who are interested in buying properties.[17] One of the side-effects of the recent pandemic is that there has been a massive increase in intrusive questions being asked as a mean of pre-qualifying prospective buyers and tenants to limit the number of viewings where there are a large number of applicants. The Irish DPC has taken the view that some of these questions involve the collection of data that is not strictly necessary for the purposes of arranging a property viewing, which is the ostensible purpose of the initial enquiry. Therefore seeking information more suited to the later stages of the process such as accepting an offer or proceeding through the conveyance are likely to

---

16 At https://www.dataprotection.ie/en/dpc-guidance/requesting-personal-data-prospective-tenants.

17 At https://www.dataprotection.ie/en/dpc-guidance/guidance-collection-personal-data-prior-viewing-property.

be seen as unnecessary and unjustifiable from a GDPR perspective.

Vital interests as a processing basis is of limited interest in the context of this book and will not be considered further. This is processing required in order to save life and prevent injury and is directed at processing by emergency services and the like. It is unlikely that processing relating to property would qualify!

Public task is a processing basis primarily of value to local and national government and governmental agencies. It allows for processing in the context of governmental work to the extent that a government body is operating within a statutory duty or power. In the property sector this would include processing for the regulation of the letting sector, planning applications, council tax collection, and benefit payments among other things. However, it is worth highlighting here that this processing basis does not mean that public bodies are exempt from the GDPR, far from it. There has been criticism of local authorities for failing to remove old planning applications from the websites and for making full details of landlords who have been granted HMO licences fully available online and not keeping them up to date. These are both breaches of the GDPR. In addition, the public task processing basis only applies to processing in support of a statutory duty. There are many things that a local authority does which involve the processing of personal data which they are not statutorily required to do.

The three key processing bases for most purposes relevant to this book are contract, legal obligation, and legitimate interests.

Contract allows for any processing required under the terms of a contractual agreement or to enable someone to enter into one. So, for a conveyancer this would authorise the taking of initial information from a prospective client in order to enter into a retainer with them. It would also authorise all the normal work involved in conveyancing their property. For an estate agent this processing basis would cover all the normal work involved in marketing a property for sale such as taking photographs and advertising it on the internet.

Legal obligation covers all forms of processing required in order to comply with the law. This means statutory obligations and anything imposed by a court order but it does not include any processing to comply with a contractual obligation. For property practitioners this would include the processing necessary to carry out anti-money laundering checks as an estate agent or conveyancer as they are required by law. It would also include selling a property where this had been ordered by a court, such as part of a divorce settlement or in an insolvency. For letting agents or landlords it would cover checks on tenants in England to comply with the Right to Rent or processing necessary to comply with the terms of a property licence or to allow for one to be applied for.

Consent is the processing basis that many Data Controllers and Data Processors default to. Under previous data protection regimes it was the most usual basis under which data was handled. It still remains important under a number of regimes around the world on the basis that consent is the clearest way to ensure that a data subject has understood and agreed with the use of their data. For example, the recent Chinese Personal Information Protection Law focuses on consent as its main mechanism for data processing. However, under the GDPR consent is not less important that before but rather no more important than any other processing basis. In practice, it is rarely the correct processing basis to use and is largely there as a backstop where no other processing basis will meet the need. Consider an example. If a conveyancer is carrying out AML checks then this will require the processing of Personal Data. However, to ask consent for this processing is to give an entirely false impression. If consent for AML processing is withheld then the conveyancer should not provide the service at all and should turn the client away. In fact, they should probably report the refusal to allow AML checks to be carried out as that is in itself suspicious. The use of consent in relation to AML checks implies that there is in fact a free choice when the choice is entirely illusory and the use of the service is intimately connected with the requirement to submit to a check, which it itself required by law. In the case of AML checks the correct processing basis is legal obligation which gives a far more accurate picture of the seriousness of the obligation and the very limited ability to refuse it. Where consent is being used it must be positive, clear, and specific. This is particularly important as it represents a substantial change from the previous regime. Under the GDPR any consent must be:

- Opt-in – the Data Subject must have explicitly agreed to the processing. That means that any form of pre-ticked box or clause in a contract that states that by signing the agreement data processing is implicitly authorised is not valid;

- Clear – consent must be separated from the main body of agreements so that it is not seen as just another part of the agreement. It must also be clearly worded and set out what processing the consent is for, who will do it, and what that processing will achieve;

- Specific – where consent is given it must be for a specific piece of data processing. It cannot be generic in nature or embrace a wide range of different processing of different pieces of data by different parties. It is likely that as a result Data Subjects who are giving consent will need to give several different consents to slightly different type of processing by different parties for different purposes. So, for example, an estate agent approached by a potential house purchaser seeking property details might need one consent for them to be added to that agent's database to be sent details of properties that would interest them, another consent to be added to the same database for other agents in the same group in nearby areas, and a further consent for the passing of that prospective buyer's details to associated mortgage brokers who might be able to assist them.

The Upper Tribunal has stated that the use of nebulous phrases such as consent being given by consumers to being given to "receive information which might interest them" is not sufficiently clear to meet the obligation for consent to be informed and will not be acceptable.[18] Therefore where consent is being relied on to market services, especially those from third parties it needs to be very explicit as to what might be marketed and in what context.

Finally, it is important to understand that consent can be withdrawn at any time and any Data Controller relying on it must have systems in place to allow this to be done easily. Of course this gives a further reason why a Data Controller would wish to use consent as a last resort as they may then have to deal with its withdrawal. Systems that deal with consent need to be designed (following the data protection by design concept) to allow for withdrawal of consent either wholly or in part. The ICO favours the use of consent management tools that permit Data Subjects to easily see what they have consented to and make adjustments to that consent in real time. If consent is given and then withdrawn but the Data Controller believes that they have an alternative processing basis then they cannot silently just carry on. They must still inform the Data Subject that they are no longer seeking to rely on consent and the alternative processing basis that they are using to justify the continued processing of data.

In addition, no service or part of it can be withheld or provided for a different price because consent has been given or withheld unless the service cannot be provided at all without that consent. So, it would be a clear breach of the GDPR to offer a discount on the provision of legal services provided that the consumer consented to having their data used for marketing purposes or sold to third party data collection agencies.

---

[18] *Leave.EU and Eldon v Information Commissioner* [2021] UKUT 26 (AAC).

## Legitimate Interests

I have deliberately separated out Legitimate Interests into its own section as it is the most complex processing basis, but also the one into which a large range of diverse items are placed. As the GDPR has come into effect, Legitimate Interests has seen a massive growth as a processing basis. This is mainly because it has been used to sweep up a wide range of matters that did not fit well into other areas and has been used to "fix" problems that were not anticipated when the legislation was drafted.

However, the use of Legitimate Interests as a wide-ranging processing basis has led to it being carefully controlled and it must be used with some caution. It is important to consider that legitimate interests could, in principle, be used to authorise almost any piece of data processing by almost anyone who could claim a need to process that data. Accordingly, this processing basis is a balance between the interests of the party claiming the legitimate interest and the interests of the Data Subject. Because it is a balance, Legitimate Interests should not be used to justify every piece of Personal Data processing, any more than any other processing basis should.

In short, Legitimate Interests allows for the processing of Personal Data which is in the interest of the Data Controller or some other identified third party. This can allow for a wide range of processing, even including some marketing activity. This may seem quite woolly but this is exactly the point. Legitimate Interests is there to allow for processing that might otherwise need consent but which would either lead to people being bombarded with long-winded consent requests, leading to what the ICO has termed "consent fatigue", or where the consent is difficult to obtain but the processing should probably happen anyway as it has a relatively low impact on the Data Subject, or may even provide a benefit to them, but is very important to the Data Controller. Therefore, a degree of flexibility is entirely appropriate because the extent to which Legitimate Interests can be relied upon is very case specific and rests on a balance being struck between the impact of a piece of processing on a Data Subject and the importance of that processing to the Data Controller and, potentially, society as a whole.

So, recital 47 to the GDPR suggests that Legitimate Interests may provide a processing basis for the Personal Data of a Data Subject where they were already in a business relationship with a Data Controller and would reasonably expect to have their data used in this way. To give some more concrete examples this approach to Legitimate Interests would allow a conveyancer to market will-writing services to its clients or an estate agent to market letting agency services to property vendors as these services would be closely connected to the original service offered and a relationship already exists between them. In fact, Legitimate Interests would permit a wide range of cross-marketing activity undertaken to persons who were already clients of the business. Marketing to third parties is also potentially permissible using Legitimate Interests provided it is low impact.

Recital 48 suggests that Legitimate Interests might also allow for data transfer between businesses that are part of the same group of companies for appropriate administrative purposes. This would allow transfer of employee data, for example, from a company that had no HR function to another group company to allow it to handle HR activities on its behalf.

The use of Legitimate Interests for marketing is currently driven by the suggestions given in the recitals to the GDPR. This does not mean that other marketing could not also be a Legitimate Interest. The ICO has indicated that it would consider marketing activity to be likely to fall within a Legitimate Interest where it was:

- low impact;
- had minimal use of Personal Data which was proportionate;

and

- would not be a surprise to people and would not be likely to lead to them objecting.

However, where marketing activity is covered by the Privacy and Electronic Communications Regulations (PECR) then Legitimate Interests is not an acceptable processing basis if those regulations require permission to be given. This will limit the use of Legitimate Interests for direct marketing to paper-based marketing as any form of electronic direct marketing is covered by PECR. So, an estate agent that has sold a property in a street could reasonably assert that Legitimate Interests would justify them sending paper-based mailshots to the remaining houses in the same street to seek other similar properties to sell. This is low impact, requires minimal use of Personal Data, and is paper-based. However, the same marketing activity undertaken using email would not be an acceptable use of Legitimate Interests as PECR does not permit this type of direct marketing without consent.

PECR does allow for direct marketing of an organisation's own services provided that there was an opportunity given to opt out of such marketing when the data was collected. So, just as Legitimate Interests would justify a conveyancing solicitor marketing a wills service to its clients, PECR would allow for this to be done by email provided that the client had been given the opportunity to opt-out of this sort of marketing at the outset. Note that PECR does not require an explicit opt-in (as the GDPR does) and allows the opt-in to be assumed (called a "soft opt-in") for this type of marketing activity.

Finally, recitals 49 and 50 expressly set out three areas that are always considered to be Legitimate Interests. These are:

1. processing of Personal Data to the extent strictly necessary to prevent fraud;

2. processing of Personal Data to ensure network and information security both in terms of preventing accidental data losses as well as detecting and preventing data theft, denial of service, unauthorised access, malware distribution, and damage to networks; and

3. identifying possible criminal acts or threats to public security by the controller and providing that information to the appropriate authorities but not if this breaches a professional or legal obligation of secrecy.

## Legitimate Interest Impact Assessments

Impact assessments are a key element of the GDPR and especially of the Legitimate Interests processing basis. Anyone using legitimate interests is encouraged to carry out an impact assessment, although there is no obligation to do so. The ICO refers to these as Legitimate Interests impact assessments (LIA's) although this is their choice of name and not one that is found in the GDPR, which only allows for the DPIA. A LIA is essentially a special purpose DPIA with a more limited scope. If the use of Legitimate Interests is more marginal and open to dispute then an impact assessment is a sensible way of showing that the issues have been considered and that any disagreement about the application of Legitimate Interests as a processing basis is a matter of interpretation and not a case of the Data Controller playing fast and loose with the GDPR.

The ICO has set out a three-step process for the carrying out of a Legitimate Interests impact assessment (LIA). This involves:

1. Identifying the Legitimate Interest. Whose interests are being protected? How are they being protected? Is there a benefit to anyone else or to society as a whole? How great are these benefits, what are their importance? What would happen if the

processing was prohibited, how serious would the consequences be? Are there any relevant laws or codes of practice which apply?

2. Setting out why the processing is necessary. How does the processing meet the identified Legitimate Interest? Could the same interest be met in a different way, ideally by processing less or no Personal Data? The more clearly the Legitimate Interest is set out (in the first step) the easier it will be to fulfil this step; and

3. Creating a balance between the identified Legitimate Interest and the rights and freedoms of the individual Data Subject. This involves considering the type of data being processed and how sensitive it is, whether there would be a reasonable expectation on the part of the Data Subject that you might process this data and what they would have known or might know about this possible use of their data. Finally, this test requires consideration of the potential impact of the processing. Will the processing mean a Data Subject will be prevented from exercising a right or accessing a service, for example?

Some examples of the considerations that are relevant on each of the three tests might be helpful:

1. The example given above of a conveyancer who then seeks to offer will-writing services to clients.

    a) The Legitimate Interests being promoted are those of the conveyancer who will obtain further work and fees from the client. There is also a benefit to the client who will have obtained a will and will have their estate more efficiently handled on death. Finally, there is a general benefit to society in having more people with professionally written wills which will reduce the number of will disputes in the courts and the workload of the Public Trustee;

b) The only way to meet the Legitimate Interest would be to process the client's personal data to contact them to have a will written. There is no other way of meeting this need or of meeting it with less data;

c) The data required for this additional marketing is only contact details so it is not especially sensitive. The client would probably not be surprised to be contacted by a professional he has previously dealt with to offer a service that is connected to his house purchase. The firm will take account of any previously expressed views on marketing and solicitation and will not contact any client who has stated that they do not want to be contacted about additional services. Lastly, the processing only seeks to offer an additional, potentially useful, service. It does not intend to create a barrier or prevent the client from accessing a service or engaging a right.

2. Looking at the other previous example of an estate agent who wishes to mailshot the owners of similar properties on the rest of a street in which he has just sold a house. Name and address data will be sourced from the Land Registry to create a personalised mailshot.

   a) The Legitimate Interest is largely that of the agent who wishes to market his services. There is a potential (small) benefit to prospective vendors who might not realise that there is an active market for their properties.

   b) The only other way that this Legitimate Interest could be met without processing personal data would be to place generic letters through the doors of every property. This would be less personalised and would potentially involve letters being sent to people with a totally different property type and to tenants who the agent is not able to assist.

c) The data being used is name and address data and information on overall size and value from the Land Registry. The agent will also check the Mail Preference Service to ensure that the mailshot is not sent to anyone who has expressed a desire not to receive unsolicited mail. Therefore there is an element of opt-out available. The receivers are unlikely to be expecting an approach and have not expressly consented to it although they may be unsurprised if they have noticed the sale of a nearby property. The data will not be retained and used beyond the immediate mailshot and so there is no longer term effect on individual rights. There is no substantial infringement on rights and no barrier to provision of services.

3. Finally, a landlord who wishes to carry out a credit reference on a prospective tenant but is not obtaining their explicit consent for this.

a) The Legitimate Interest is primarily that of the landlord in having a tenant who will be able to afford the rent for her property and is likely to be able to continue to afford it. There is a societal benefit as well in ensuring that individuals do not take on liabilities that they cannot afford and so end up in debt. There is also a potential benefit in terms of helping to reduce fraud by individuals who might seek to conceal their identity or means to rent a property that they cannot afford.

b) A credit check is one of the most common ways of establishing affordability. Similar information could be derived by asking for details of the prospective tenant's employer and approaching them for an employer's reference. However, this would be more intrusive and would involve the employer knowing about the prospective tenant's housing plans.

c) The data being used is relatively sensitive in that it involves personal financial standing. However, a credit reference is common in property rentals and so a tenant is unlikely to be surprised that this is being done. The tenant will be told that a credit check will be carried out. The tenant is potentially going to be refused a service however as if they have insufficiently good credit they will not be offered the tenancy.

None of these examples goes so far as to draw a conclusion but they each set out the type of considerations that would go into an LIA. The ICO template has boxes for each test and then a final box to set out reasons why the Legitimate Interests processing basis should or should not be accepted. In each example this would allow for a final consideration of the balance between the interest and the Data Subject's rights. For all the examples above the intrusion on Data Subject rights is either minimal or, in the case of the tenant, justified by the Legitimate Interest to be protected.

## Changing Processing Bases

It is important to understand that data processing bases are not monolithic. So, a single interaction between a Data Controller and a Data Subject can move through a range of processing bases as different data is processed for different purposes during that interaction. In some cases one processing basis will fall away and be replaced by another as the relationship evolves. In other cases two or more processing bases may exist simultaneously but be applicable to different pieces of Personal Data. This is often hard to understand and so a more detailed example might be appropriate.

An estate agent who has sold a property on a street might decide to carry out a paper-based direct marketing exercise to other property owners on the same street using name and address data obtained from the Land Registry. This would be direct marketing under the basis of Legitimate Interests. As a result of this marketing the estate agent is contacted by Mr Jones who wishes to obtain a valuation. The agent obtains some details in order to carry out a free valuation. This data is obtained and processed on the basis of contract as it is pre-contractual enquiries. After the valuation the estate agent retains the data again on the basis of Legitimate Interests in order to protect its position if the valuation is questioned. After two months the estate agent has heard nothing more and so contacts Mr Jones again to see if he is still interested. This is further marketing activity which is again on the basis of Legitimate Interests as Mr Jones has been in a previous business relationship and would reasonably expect a further contact. Mr Jones says he is planning to sell and instructs the estate agent to sell the property for him on its usual terms. He also says he is looking to buy somewhere else and is seeking a mortgage to help with this. The estate agent enters into a contract with Mr Jones and processes his data on the basis of that contract. It uses this basis to advertise the property on suitable property portals and to instruct third parties (with whom it has appropriate data processing agreements) to carry out an EPC and take photographs of the property. The estate agent also carries out the statutorily required AML checks using the legal obligation processing basis to fulfil its legal requirement to do those checks. The estate agent has a group company which is a mortgage broker and using the Legitimate Interests processing basis it passes Mr Jones' details on to that company for them to make an approach to him for assistance in finding a mortgage. A buyer is then found and Mr Jones' is introduced to another group company offering conveyancing services. This conveyancer enters into a contract with Mr Jones and processes his data using the contract processing basis. It carries out its own AML checks using the legal obligation processing basis. On completion of the sale the conveyancer files transfer papers with the Land Registry who process the data to update the land ownership register on the basis of public task as it is fulfilling a statutory function. At the end of the conveyancing process the conveyancer archives the files for a period of six years on the basis of a legitimate interest in protecting itself from future claims. The conveyancer then markets will writing services to Mr Jones as a person whose asset base has recently altered. This marketing is again on the basis of legitimate interests as there is an ongoing business relationship which Mr Jones might reasonably expect to involve him being advised of additional relevant services.

This example shows how the estate agent and conveyancer have carried out different processing on the basis of Legitimate Interest, Contract, and Legal Obligation and shows that there has been a process of change between those processing basis as the relationship between Mr Jones and the estate agent and then Mr Jones and the conveyancer evolves from him being a marketing prospect to being a client, and then to a former client.

## Special Category Data

Some Personal Data is especially sensitive. Naturally it is all sensitive to some degree and some types of Personal Data are more important than others but some data is treated as especially sensitive by the GDPR. This especially sensitive data is called Special Category Data under the GDPR. Under the old data protection regime it used to be called Sensitive Personal Data. Special Category Data includes Personal Data which reveals a Data Subject's:

- racial or ethnic origin;
- political opinions;

- religious or philosophical beliefs;
- trade union membership;
- genetic information;
- biometric information used for identity verification;
- health; and
- sex life or sexual orientation.

Data about criminal offences and convictions are not Special Category but there is a separate category for this data which means that the rules around it are very similar to those for Special Category Data.

It is important to note that a number of things are not included. For example, financial data such as bank records or credit card details are not Special Category and neither are important identity information such as my passport or driver's licence number. That does not mean that this data is not important and should not be treated with a great deal of care. The GDPR expects that Personal Data will be segmented and more security applied to more important Personal Data. However, Special Category Data is more directed toward data which needs my particular permission, or an important justification, in order to justify its processing. The main point is that Special Category Data is information which could lead to a Data Subject being victimised or their rights being abused if it were processed maliciously or inappropriately secured. Some of the items on the list make clear the European nature of the legislation. For example, while trade unions have often had a difficult relationship with government and employers in the UK, being a member of a union has not historically led to substantial victimisation. In other European countries, with a more violent recent political history, trade union membership has led to intimidation, imprisonment, and murder at the hands of the state. Therefore its inclusion in the list speaks as much to a European fear of this information being abused as opposed to a pattern of misuse in the UK. Special Category Data is a bit of a grab-bag of data about a person's inner mental life such as their beliefs and views as well as specific data about their biological makeup such as their health, genetic and biometric information. The focus on genetic and biometric data is also a key element of the GDPR as it seeks to bring the data protection regime into the modern age by seeking to protect such things as our individual genetic makeup.

When this book was originally conceived it seemed unlikely that property lawyers and property professionals would seem overly concerned with Special Category Data, or at any rate that they would have any real justification for being concerned with it. However, during the recent outbreak of novel Coronavirus the health of individuals became a key issue for property managers who had repairing obligations as they were being advised by the government not to carry out any but the most critical repairs and maintenance in properties where a person was being require to isolate themselves because they may be carrying the virus or where a person was shielding themselves because they were uniquely vulnerable to the effects of the virus. This implicitly required the recording of health data, which is Special Category Data.

First, there must be a specific processing basis that justifies the collection of the Special Category Data. A list of these is set out in the Data Protection Act 2018. The processing basis that applies in this case is one of a group of public interest bases and specifically is the processing basis which allows collection for the purpose of safeguarding individuals at risk.

Second, Special Category Data can only be collected if the party collecting it has an appropriate written policy which allows for this to be done. The ICO provides an outline policy document for this purpose [https://ico.org.uk/media/for-organisations/documents/2616286/appropriate-policy-document.docx] which gives a checklist of information and items that can be completed to create a satisfactory written policy.

Third, appropriate security must be in place. Special Category Data is far more sensitive than ordinary personal data and should have greater security applied to it. For larger organisations it is important to consider whether this type of data needs to be available to everyone. For example, accounts staff will need to know about rent payment data but will have little need to be acquainted with health data and so should not routinely have access to this.

Finally, consideration will need to be given to deleting this data. Once the current emergency is over there is no need to maintain records on who did or did not have coronavirus symptoms and so it is important to be clear about how this data will be deleted and ensure that there is a process to allow this to be done easily and securely.

The same issues will apply over the longer term in relation to vaccine data. It may be that there will be a longer term need to retain data relating to vaccine status of employees or other parties. This data will be health data and so protected as special category data and so the processing rules above will apply.

# CHAPTER FOUR

# DATA PROCESSORS AND CONTROLLERS

One of the key elements of the GDPR is who is responsible for complying with the regulations. The GDPR splits data handlers into Data Controllers and Data Processors. These are crucial definitions as they have different obligations.

A Data Controller is a party who decides how personal data is processed. A Data Processor by contrast is someone who does the actual processing but at the behest of a Controller. This needs some careful consideration. A Data Controller can also be the processor of that data, there is no requirement to have some other processor. A Data Processor however must always have another party who is the Data Controller. In other words, a Data Controller is required for every piece of personal data, a Data Processor is optional.

Sometimes it can be hard to work out who is who. The key point is to consider who decides how the data is processed. If a party has a decision-making power in terms of how the data is processed and who does that processing then they are likely to be the Data Controller. A party that merely processes data by way of an agreement with someone else and can be replaced is likely to be a Data Processor.

So, for example, an estate agent will be the Data Controller in respect of the Personal Data of their vendor clients and of prospective purchasers. They might choose to keep all that data in a mixture of paper filing cabinets and electronic records stored on their own office computers. However, they might also store all their data in an online document cloud service provided by a third party. In that case the third party would be the Data Processor. They would only be storing and handling the data at the behest of the estate agent and the estate agent could, in principle, remove them and get some other cloud service run by someone else. In this scenario the estate agent would not be holding any data themselves, it would all be in the possession of the Data Processor but the estate agent would remain the Data Controller.

The identification of parties can be made even more difficult where there are two or more Data Controllers who control data together. In these cases, the Data Controllers may be Joint Controllers. Joint Controller situations should be distinguished from cases where the same, or similar, data is being handled by several unconnected parties for a similar purpose. A Joint Controller situation involves a much tighter connection than this. So, for example, an estate agent and a conveyancing solicitor will be processing very similar personal data about their mutual client, the property vendor, and will be doing so for the same purpose, the sale of the client's property. However, they will be using their own independent databases to do so and will be handling the Personal Data they hold entirely separately. However, if the estate agent also owns a mortgage broker this might be a separate legal entity but share a database with the estate agent firm and process the data in tandem with the estate agent firm, using the same data processing policies and operating jointly for marketing purposes. In this case the estate agent and mortgage broker would be Joint Controllers of the Personal Data.

## Data Controllers

The reason that the Data Controller/Data Processor distinction is important is that the liability for compliance with the GDPR falls primarily on the Data Controller. Data Controllers must comply with the data protection principles and be able to show that compliance. They must also pay the relevant data protection fees to the ICO. Data Processors are not exempt from control and the ICO, or other appropriate supervisory body and individuals can still take action against them for breaches of the GDPR, but their obligations are much reduced. In particular Data Processors have very limited responsibility for ensuring that Personal Data is being collected in accordance with the GDPR and is being used in accordance with a lawful processing basis as they are primarily engaged on processing in the manner that they have been instructed to by the Data Controller.

The Data Controller is therefore primarily liable for complying with the full sweep of the GDPR obligations. Even if the Data Controller is not actively processing Personal Data and has arranged for a Data Processor to do this on their behalf, the Data Controller remains primarily liable for compliance with the GDPR. Those core obligations are:

- Complying with the GDPR data protection principles;
- Complying with the Accountability principle;
- Ensuring that Data Subjects are able to exercise the rights given to them by the GDPR;
- Implementing appropriate security for Personal Data in terms of both technical security and organisational security procedures;
- Using a suitable Data Processor;
- Entering into a suitable binding contract with a Data Processor which complies with the GDPR;
- Complying with the restrictions on data transfers outside the UK or EEA;
- Having a representative inside the UK or EEA (for Data

Controllers based outside the UK or EEA respectively);

- Co-operating with the appropriate data protection supervisor;
- Paying the appropriate data protection registration fee to the ICO.

Where Data Controllers are Joint Controllers their responsibility for the handling of Personal Data is shared and co-equal. Collectively the Joint Controllers must meet all the obligations set out above and they can divide those obligations between them. However, a data protection supervisor or a Data Subject can hold either Joint Controller responsible for any failure. Joint Controllers are required to clearly split their obligations as Data Controllers between themselves and to do so transparently so that Data Subjects can obtain, in writing, the details of that split. They are particularly required to be clear about which of them will be responsible for each of an individual's Data Protection Rights. There is no obligation to have a contract between Joint Controllers but given that they are each fully liable for any failure by the other it would be sensible to do so.

## Data Processors

Data Processors have far fewer obligations under the GDPR than Data Controllers. Many of these are set out in the compulsory agreement that the Data Processor must have with the Data Controller (see below). The key obligations are as follows:

- Acting only on the Data Controller's instructions- Data Processors act only in accordance with instructions from a Data Controller. If a Data Processor processes Personal Data without such instructions then they become a Data Controller in respect of that processing activity. In practice a Data Processor who did this would be at very high risk indeed of breaching the GDPR as they would likely be carrying out processing without any lawful basis and without having given appropriate information to the Data Subject.

- Formal contract- Data Processors are obligated by the GDPR to enter into formal written contracts with Data Controllers (see below).

- Sub-processors- Data Processors must process Personal Data entirely within their own organisation. They are only permitted to use sub-contractors or sub-processors with explicit consent in advance. This consent may be generic in nature and, in practice, often is. Even where permission is given to use a sub-processor the Data Processor is under obligations to ensure that the sub-processor provides the same protections to Personal Data as the Data Processor provides.

- Security- implementing appropriate technical and organisational measures to protect Personal Data.

- Notification of breaches- Data Processors have an obligation under the GDPR to notify the relevant Data Controller of a data breach without "undue delay". A Data Controller/Data Processor contract may impose a shorter timeline. if you become aware of a personal data breach, you must notify the relevant controller without undue delay.

- Notification of potential GDPR breaches- a Data Processor must inform a Data Controller immediately if they give an instruction which will lead to a breach of the GDPR or the DPA 18.

- Accountability obligations: you must comply with certain GDPR accountability obligations, such as maintaining records and appointing a data protection officer. For more information please read our guidance on accountability and governance.

- Personal Data transfers outside the EEA- Data Processors have the same limits on transferring data outside the EEA as Data Controllers

- Appointing a representative within the UK or EEA- Data Processors established outside the UK or EEA must have a representative inside the UK or EEA respectively.

- Cooperation with data protection supervisors- As with Data Controllers, Data Processors must cooperate with the relevant data protection supervisor

**Data Controller/Processor agreements**

Because the GDPR was always intended to work across multiple European Countries with differing legal systems it relies heavily on contractual relationships on the basis that these are similar in all the relevant jurisdictions and also similar elsewhere. Any Data Processor who is instructed to process Personal Data by Data Controller is required by the GDPR to enter into a legally enforceable agreement, normally a contractual one. This requirement also solves the issues of enforceability as it makes it the responsibility of the controller and processor to ensure that their relationship is legally enforceable in whatever legal jurisdiction applies to it. Thus, an organisation can be held responsible for compliance with the GDPR and for ensuring that there is a binding controller/processor contract even if that contract is covered by the law of a country far outside the EEA. The GDPR specifies in relatively general terms the things that must be in these contracts but leaves it up to the parties to choose the wording and to ensure that they have incorporated the points properly. This is intended to ensure that both parties comply with the GDPR and that individual Personal Data is properly protected. It is important to note that if a Data Processor uses a sub-processor to fulfil any part of their agreement with the Data Controller another similar agreement must be entered into that also meets the specifications of the GDPR and provides the same level of protection for Personal Data as the original contract between the Data Controller and Data Processor does.

Data Controller/Data Processor agreements are required to do the following things:

- Set out the details of the processing that is to be carried out including:
    - What Personal Data is being processed exactly and why;
    - How the Personal Data is going to be processed;
    - Whose Personal Data is being processed in a general sense, by category;
    - How long the processing is to carry on for;
- Specify what the Data Controller is required to do and what rights they have;
- Require the Data Processor to only act based on instructions form the Data Controller unless they are under a legal obligation to do something. Those instructions must be recorded in a written form but they can be given in any form that can be kept;
- Require the Data Processor to ensure that anyone processing Personal Data for the Data Controller is themselves obligated

to keep the data confidential. This includes employees and any temporary or agency workers or contracted staff;

- Require the Data Processor to take the appropriate steps to secure the Personal Data. In fact, the obligation to secure data applies equally to the Data Controller and the Data Processor under the GDPR but the Data Controller/Data Processor agreement only binds the Data Processor to secure Personal Data. This security includes the full range of measures including securing the data from unauthorised access by technical and physical measures (ie. passwords, encryption, locks etc), ensuring resilience of the Personal Data by preventing unauthorised alteration, corruption, and making sure it remains accessible and available, keeping backups and being able to restore data access promptly after an incident, and testing to ensure that these measures are effective. Security is a substantial issue in relation to the GDPR as ultimately poor computer security is a key factor in many data losses. The ICO has produced quite substantial guidance to computer security issues within its GDPR pages discussing what they consider to be the most important issues in computer security.[19] Any organisation processing personal data using computers should consider this guidance carefully and should also consider applying for one of the UK government approved standards such as Cyber-Essentials to help demonstrate their commitment to computer security;

- Prohibiting the Data Processor from engaging any sub-processor without explicit consent from the Data Controller in advance and also requiring the Data Processor to enter into

[19] At https://ico.org.uk/for-organisations/guide-to-data-protection/guide-to-the-general-data-protection-regulation-gdpr/security/

written contracts with any authorised sub-processors.

- Requiring the Data Processor to do anything appropriate to assist the Data Controller in complying with its GDPR obligations such as responding to Data Subjects seeking to exercise their GDPR rights, notification of data breaches, and data protection impact assessments;

- Requiring the Data Processor to delete or return any Personal Data they hold at the end of the agreement;

- Compelling the Data Processor to allow for audits and inspections by the Data Controller or their appropriate nominees.

In January 2020, the EDPB approved standard clauses in English for a Data Controller/Data Processor agreement which were produced by the Danish data protection supervisory body. There is no obligation to use these clauses but doing so is considered as being likely to meet the requirements of the GDPR. At the time of writing the ICO has not produced its own such clauses and refers to the Danish ones as suitable for use. The main problem with the Danish clauses is that they are extremely wordy, extending to nineteen pages, probably longer than many of the contracts they are to be inserted into. It would in fact be possible to achieve much the same effect in just three or four pages. The ICO may in time produce its own, shorter, clauses and the general comments made by the UK government and the ICO about simplifying the GDPR in practice would tend to suggest that this is something that is being considered.

These are the bare minimum requirements of a controller/processor agreement. There is no reason why they cannot do far more. For example, a Data Processor might agree to deal with many of the responsibilities that the legislation places on a Data Controller, such as the giving of a privacy notice. This is no different from many similar contractual agreements, such as agency relationships, where the agent agrees contractually to deal with statutory obligations which bind their principal.

It can often be hard to work out who is the Data Controller and who is the Data Processor. For example, consider the case of property management agents. They often erroneously view themselves as Data Controllers leading to problems such as agents taking an overly-enthusiastic view of the GDPR and then refusing to release information about a landlord's own tenants to that landlord.

At first glance, it might appear that a property management company would be a Data Controller, as its client, the property owner, will often hold little or no information and the property management company will deal with everything on its behalf. However, this misunderstands the roles of Data Controller and Data Processor.

A Data Controller, despite the title, is not the party in physical possession or direct control of the data. It refers instead to their capacity to decide how the data shall be handled, and by whom. Therefore, a Data Controller does not need to be in possession of personal data or even have day to day access to it. It is a Data Controller because it ultimately has the power to decide who will handle the relevant personal data on its behalf.

A property management company will usually not have that level of control and this will normally will be set out in the agreement between the manager and the owner. While a manager might handle the data for the owner often with little or no oversight, it does not in fact have a complete right to dispose of that data and the owner could, in principle, dispense with the services of the manager at any time, recover the personal data held by the manager, and then have a new manager process the date instead. It is this ability to replace the manager which makes the owner the Data Controller, rather than the manager.

Accordingly, a pure property management company will not be a Data Controller simply because it manages property for a property owner. However a property manager may be holding personal data in its own right as a Data Controller. So, if a property manager is managing property for individuals, rather than companies, then it will be holding their personal data and be a Data Controller in respect of it.

# CHAPTER FIVE

# DATA SUBJECT RIGHTS

One of the most important elements of the GDPR is the awarding of rights to Data Subjects. Almost every other part of the GDPR is leading up to this point in that they are either dictating who it is that is required to acknowledge and make provision for these rights or ensuring they are enforceable. The concept of Data Subject rights is fundamental to the inherent tension which the GDPR is always seeking to resolve. The GDPR, quite intentionally, does not give Data Subjects ownership over their data. This is something that privacy advocates have sought for some time and was one of the things that they wanted from the EU. However, the EU deliberately did not take this course as to do so would have undermined companies that had invested money and energy in creating valuable databases. These databases would have been rendered worthless overnight if the organisations concerned no longer owned the data within them. In order to resolve this tension, the GDPR does not disturb the ownership of data and instead creates a new series of rights which mimic many of the qualities of ownership without in fact creating ownership of data. These rights are primarily exercisable by a Data Subject as against the Data Controller. Data Processors may be asked by the Data Controller to assist where a Data Subject has sought to exercise a right but the primary obligation to meet that request rests with the Data Controller. The Data Processor is being asked to assist on the strength of the Data Controller/Data Processor contract. The key rights of Data Subjects under the GDPR are the:

- right to transparent information
- right of access

- right to rectification
- right to erasure (also called the "right to be forgotten")
- right to restriction of data processing
- right to data portability
- right to object
- right to information about and to object to automated decision making and profiling.

Some of these rights are relatively simple while some are far more complex and require significant changes in practice. Each of them will be dealt with in turn below.

## The Right to Transparent Information

This is a key element of the GDPR on which its value to individuals largely stands or falls. There is little point in giving individual Data Subjects rights if they have no idea that these exist, that they have been engaged, and who they can be exercised against. The right to transparent information, or the right to be informed as the ICO tends to call it, is key to enabling this.

The GDPR requires that a Data Controller provides clear and transparent information to a Data Subject that in broad terms tells a Data Subject in relation to their Personal Data:

- **who** is collecting and handling it;
- **what** is being done with it;

- the **legal basis** for that collection and processing; and
- **how long** they will be keeping it.

In more detail, there is a specific requirement to give a Data Subject a set of information at the time their Personal Data is collected. This is usually referred to as a privacy notice. A privacy notice needs to give a Data Subject the following information:

- The details of the organisation acting as Data Controller and who is giving the notice along with its contact details;
- The details of any data protection officer if the organisation has one;
- The purpose of processing;
- The lawful basis for the processing and the legitimate interests if this is the processing basis being relied on;
- Any other party who will receive Personal Data such as a Data Processor;
- Details of any data transfer to a third country, especially one outside the UK or EEA;
- The retention periods for the personal data
- The data subject's rights around data processing. Most organisations refer to the ICO website for this in practice;
- That the data subject has a right to remove or limit consent for data processing. This is usually expressed briefly in a single

sentence and often linked with a reference to the data subject's other rights;

- The right to lodge a complaint with the ICO or other relevant data protection supervisor; and

- Whether there is an obligation to allow the processing of Personal Data, in a statute or contract. In practice, this is usually dealt with as part of the purpose and lawful basis.

It is important to bear in mind that there is an obligation as well to keep this information clear and in plain language. The ICO is clear that this means that a privacy notice should avoid jargon and not be excessively long. There has been significant criticism of some corporate privacy notices for being so long that no reasonable individual is likely to read them. This is far from the objective of the GDPR. One of the key problems with most longer privacy notices is that they tend to go into far too much detail. This is, to some degree, the fault of the ICO, which has encouraged data maps to be used to create privacy notices. Inevitably, if a data map is produced with a significant amount of data flow it will be complex. If it is then rendered into a privacy notice that notice will itself be long and complex. There is also the natural fear of organisations when seeking to deal with a new area of law with limited guidance which means that they have a tendency to make sure that the privacy notice covers all possible bases to protect themselves from any risk of criticism. However, this is to misunderstand the purpose of a privacy notice within the GDPR and to, again, fail to appreciate that the GDPR is far more focused more on end goals than the actual methods used to achieve them. Data Subjects do not need to be told in exhaustive detail every potential use of their data. They need to be told broadly what is being done with it and why. Therefore a more general description of the uses and purposes of processing is perfectly acceptable.

A privacy notice can be provided on paper but it is more usual to provide it electronically. It can be linked from a webpage. The GDPR prefers this as the recitals make clear. Likely, because it allows for it to be searched easily. The ICO requires that such a link is reasonably prominent, in a contrasting font, and given a title that makes clear what it is about such as "data privacy notice" or "your data rights".

There is a common misconception that a privacy notice is some form of contract and that this prevents it being changed. It is not. It is nothing more than a piece of information provided in text form and so a Data Controller can alter it at any time to reflect a change in the way in which they process data. Indeed, they are positively expected to do so. Many organisations make this clear by including a statement within the privacy notice that it is subject to change at any time and that Data Subjects should review it regularly.

## The Right of Access

The right of access to Personal Data is really just the ability to make a subject access request as found in the previous data privacy regime updated for the GDPR. These can be made to the Data Controller and it is their obligation to comply with them. If the request is made to a Data Processor then it is still the Data Controller of that Personal Data who must comply but they may have a contractual arrangement with the Data Processor which allows them to ask the Data Processor to deal with the request. The final obligation to comply however always rests with the Data Controller.

There are three different types of access request that the GDPR allows for:

1. A simple confirmation that a Data Controller is processing their data at all. The answer to such a request is a plain "yes" or "no";

2. A copy of the Personal Data that is being processed. This is the same as under the previous data protection regime;

3. Further supplemental information. This is essentially the same information as is required to be in a privacy notice and so most organisations will simply supply this.

Unlike the previous regime no charge can be made in respect of an access request. More importantly, there is no specific format for making such a request and it can be made by any valid communication medium to any staff member, even in a telephone call or through social media. So a client of a conveyancing firm could simply call that firm and ask the receptionist who answers the call to provide their Personal Data. Therefore it is important that organisations have trained their staff to recognise subject access requests and to respond to them. To add to the complexity there is nothing to prevent a third party making an access request on behalf of a specific Data Subject either, provided it is with their consent. So a solicitor might make a request on behalf of a client or a parent on behalf of a child. There is no set format for obtaining consent and so a Data Controller will need to have some process for deciding whether there is reasonable evidence of consent for an access request.

It is not possible to limit the rights of Data Subjects by insisting that access requests be made in a specific way or that evidence of third-party consent is provided in a specific format. However, the GDPR recommends, in its recitals, that mechanisms are provided for making subject access requests electronically, such as an electronic form. So Data Controllers are encouraged to provide an electronic mechanism for making a request but they cannot insist on it being used and must still recognise and action requests made in other ways.

Access requests must be complied with within one calendar month of being made, shorter than the 40 days allowed under the previous regime. This means that in some months, such as February, there will be less time for the request to be actioned. It is possible to extend time for a further two months in exceptional cases if the request is very complex or the same person has sent multiple requests. However, this is exceptional and it is not permissible to simply state for every request that it will take additional time. If you are asking for identity information to confirm the identity of a person making a request then the one month timeline runs from the date that this information is provided. So, for example, a surveyor receives a request to provide a copy of Personal Data held by them on 16 January. They ask for some identity information and this is received on 31 January. They start counting the time from that day, which is the last day of January, so the Personal Data sought must be provided by the last day of February, 28 February (29 February if it is a leap year!).

If a request is excessive, unfounded or it is a repeated request then it is permissible to charge a fee. This can be the reasonable administrative costs of complying with the request. The government can place a cap on the level of that reasonable fee but have not done so to date. It is also permissible to refuse an excessive or unfounded request as well. Generally this allows for the refusal of requests that are being made to harass or intimidate or where the subject is not truly interested in exercising their rights. The ICO has indicated that it would be likely to be acceptable to refuse a request where that request was accompanied by an offer to withdraw it for a collateral benefit (because the person is not really seeking to exercise their GDPR rights) or where that request is in the context of or accompanied by a statement that it is to cause disruption or involves an unsubstantiated accusation. An excessive request is not judged based on whether it imposes a burden on the Data Controller. It is more likely that a request is excessive if it is repeated and simply asks for the same data as a previous request, especially if the data does not change regularly. If a request is substantial it is open to a Data Controller to seek to clarify the terms of the request but if you are seeking to clarify a request in order to reduce or limit its scope the one month clock for response is not stalled by this and so you are still required to respond within the one month time limit. It is also important to note that under the old regime the 40-day period was generally honoured more "in the breach" and was often treated somewhat as a guideline than as a strict time limit. The view from the ICO is that they will treat the one-month time limit under the GDPR far more strictly and so it is important that these time limits are being met. It would also be a breach of the accountability principle for data not to be organised and managed so that timelines for subject access requests can be reasonably met and so excuses for failing to meet the deadlines are difficult to justify. However, it should be noted that the Law Society has taken the view that an access request cannot be refused on the basis that a solicitor is holding a lien over papers in order to obtain settlement of an invoice. So a subject access request potentially overrides a lien. This means that a lien is now largely limited to papers belonging to companies and other entities who cannot assert GDPR rights.

However, a DSAR is limited to seeking personal data. This is misunderstood by many of those seeking data who think that they can use a DSAR to obtain documents, often to further a wider agenda or seek information to establish a claim they believe exists. However, a DSAR does not give an automatic right to access documents. When a DSAR is responded to there will be several classes of documentary information. There will be:

- documents which wholly consist of personal information which are disclosable in full;
- documents which contain some personal information but which also contain other material which relates to others or which is not personal information. Those documents may be disclosable with redaction of the other material if the personal information is a significant part of the document;
- documents which contain only a passing mention of the Data Subject or which are exempt from disclosure for some other

reason (see below).

For documents in the third category it is perfectly acceptable to simply inform the Data Subject that identified categories of personal data appeared in a specific number of documents but that those documents only contained a passing reference to them. So, for example, an employee who requests all documents referring to them would potentially have a large number of emails which they were their name appeared as they sent, received, or were copied into the exchange. A DSAR reply to them which related to those emails might say:

> "Your name appeared in 587 emails in which you were the sender, receiver, or were copied into the exchange. No other personal information was in those emails."

The key point to note is that the right being exercised is to be informed of the personal information that an organisation has obtained and used, not to be given copies of every document an organisation might have that has a mention of the Data Subject.

For example, a property litigator that has evicted a homeowner and repossessed a property on behalf of a mortgage company with an unpaid charge is approached by the other side who suggests that they have committed fraud because the mortgage was improperly made despite this issue already having been considered and dismissed by the courts at first instance and on an attempted appeal. The party demands access to papers using a GDPR subject access request and also says it will be complaining to the SRA. The party suggests that they will withdraw all the complaints if the firm pays them the sum of £25,000 which they assert they have lost due to the alleged fraud. It would be reasonable to refuse this access request as it is an unfounded request. It is based on an attempt to obtain money at threat of a time-consuming request so the individual is less interested in obtaining their rights than in obtaining funds. In addition, the request is unfounded as it is part of a campaign of complaint based on assertions that the courts have already ruled as without basis.

The Courts have taken a robust approach to refusals where the Data Subject has made a request which is clearly intended to be a nuisance rather than a legitimate exercise of their rights. In *Lees v Lloyds Bank Plc*[20] the High Court dismissed a claim for damages for refusal to answer a DSAR. There the High Court made clear that it had a discretion to make orders for disclosure or damages in support of a DSAR. It highlighted the following factors as reasons to refuse to exercise the discretion:

1. Mr Lees had issued a large number of DSARs which were repetitive in nature;

2. It was quite clear that Mr Lees was using the DSARs to obtain documents that he thought would support a legal claim rather than obtain his personal data;

3. The DSARs were being used for a collateral purpose which was to try to frustrate a mortgage possession claim. This was not a reason to refuse in itself but it was a key factor;

4. The fact that the data that was being sought would provide no benefit as there was a total legal defence to his claim and the issue had already been decided by lower courts and all appeals had been exhausted.

This case does not mean that every DSAR which has similar characteristics can be rejected. No one factor above is enough to refuse a DSAR but a combination of them is likely to be. So a Data Subject making repeated requests for the same data which is clearly intended to obtain something more than their personal data for some other purpose is very likely to be making a request that can be legitimately

---

[20] *Lees v Lloyds Bank Plc* [2020] EWHC 2249 (Ch)

rejected.

If a request is to be refused then there is an obligation to say that you are doing so and to give the reasons why in writing. You must also tell the requester that they are able to complain to a data protection supervisor, the ICO in most cases, or take their complaint to the courts. In practice, this usually then results in a complaint to the ICO.

Under the previous regime there was a substantial escape clause within subject access requests in that it was generally possible to avoid providing any data that could be classed as Personal Data of a third party. The GDPR has no such blanket exemption and takes a far more nuanced approach.

The DPA 18 does allow for refusal to provide information where it would involve disclosing any information about someone else who can be identified from that information. This includes disclosing that the other person was the source of information and also includes situations where the information to be disclosed coupled with some other piece of information that the Data Controller would reasonably expect the requester to hold would be sufficient to identify a person. So, for example, disclosing data that did not name a person but which identified the company they worked for and their job function would be sufficient to identify them if job functions were likely to be known to the requester or were publicly available knowledge. However, this limit is qualified. However, the data can be disclosed if the third party has consented to that disclosure or if it is "reasonable to do so". It is not acceptable to simply refuse to disclose data simply because it came from a third party, it is a matter that needs to be considered in each case. When assessing reasonableness the DPA 18 states that it is necessary to consider:

- What type of information you are being asked to disclose. In other words, how sensitive is the information about the third party. It might merely identify them or it might involve much more personal information;

- Whether there is any specific duty of confidentiality owed to the third party;

- Whether there has been any attempt to obtain the consent of the third party and whether they can give that consent;

- Whether there has been any specific refusal of consent by that third party.

In practice, what this means is balancing the rights of the requester as against the third party. While the DPA 18 does not mention these factors this means that a consideration is likely to include:

- Whether the third party has acted properly or has breached the law or the procedures of the Data Controller or the data sought discloses some other wrongdoing;

- How sensitive and important the data is to the requester.

There is also an exemption relating to confidential references which gives a blanket exemption from disclosure of any reference given in confidence for employment purposes, appointment to any office, or the provision of services by a Data Subject.

It is open to a Data Controller to ask for identity information when a request is made for information. However, the ICO is clear that this is only to be used in cases of doubt and a Data Controller cannot have a policy of always asking for identity information as this will put an unnecessary barrier in the way of Data Subjects. So, for example, where a law firm is conveyancing a property for an individual and they have been corresponding with the fee earner concerned by email and they then from the same email address make an access request which the fee earner then confirms by calling the telephone number held for that client on file there is very little basis for then seeking identity information from the same person.

## Right of Rectification

This right is one of the simplest and is a straight carry over from the previous regime. Data Subjects always have a right to have incorrect Personal Data corrected. In practice, most organisations want to keep data up to date as it is of limited use to them if it is wrong.

As with an access request, a request for rectification of data can be made to anyone and through any communications mechanism. So, as with access requests a certain amount of staff awareness is necessary.

There is a time limit of one calendar month to rectify data as with an access request and it is calculated in exactly the same way. However, if Personal Data was being used to make important decisions that would have far reaching effects on the Data Subject then the data should be corrected more quickly, and certainly before any decision is made. However, it should be noted that the Data Subject can seek a restriction on processing while the accuracy of Personal Data is determined. Again, as with an access request the time to rectify can be extended by a further two months in extreme cases.

When a request is received then the Data Controller must take reasonable steps to confirm the data is accurate and then amend it if necessary. The amount of effort required to investigate the accuracy is dependent on the sensitivity and importance of the data. If it is a matter of a misspelled name then the level of investigation required is minimal and the accuracy should, in any event, be easy to determine. However, a more complex and more sensitive correction, such as an assertion that an entire fact-find was wrong, would require far more careful investigation. While you are investigating a statement of inaccuracy it is good practice not to use the data to make any decision that relies on the uncertain data. The Data Subject can in any event make a request for restriction of processing to prevent processing while a rectification request is considered.

Where the Data Controller considers the data to be accurate then they may refuse to rectify it. In that case they must inform the Data Subject that the Personal Data will not be rectified, the reasons for this and that there is a right to complain to the relevant supervisory body. The ICO considers it good practice to note that a request was made and the reasons for refusal.

If data is inaccurate but the mistake is already known and has been corrected then it could be argued that the mistaken data is subject to rectification. However, the ICO considers that provided the erroneous data has been corrected then the recording of the previously wrong data alongside the note that it is wrong is actually accurate data and it should be retained as a more accurate reflection of events. Likewise if Personal Data contains an opinion that is not agreed or that has been modified over time then the retention of that opinion, provided that it is clearly marked as such, is an accurate reflection of the Personal Data and its evolution over time and so the opinion should not be deleted.

For example, a team of property litigation solicitors are working on a case. One of them records an opinion in an attendance note that the client is likely to be a poor witness in court because he tends to change his story under cross-examination to fit what he believes the case should be. The client ultimately gives live evidence at trial and his account is accepted by the Court. However, the client finds out about the note and insists it is deleted as it is not accurate. The solicitor's firm refuses deletion. The note was ultimately shown to be incorrect as the file demonstrates. However, it was clearly expressed as an opinion and was validly held. The inaccuracy of the opinion in the circumstances is shown by the file. Therefore, taken as a whole the

Personal Data in the file is accurate.

As with access requests it is possible to refuse rectification requests that are repeated or unfounded. The criteria for these is essentially the same as for refusal of an access request but the most obvious example is where a Data Subject makes repeated requests for the same data to be rectified. Again, as with an access request where a rectification request is made repetitively or is excessive a fee can be charged.

The position on seeking further identity information is the same for a rectification request as it is for an access request. Identity information cannot be sought as a matter of routine and should only be asked for if there is some reason to doubt the identity of the person making the rectification request.

If the Data Controller has supplied Personal Data to another organisation then if they rectify that data they must also inform all the organisations who have received the data and ask them to make the same corrections. For example, an estate agent has obtained Personal Data from their client. They have passed that data to a group company which offers mortgage broking services. The client then asks for rectification of some of the Personal Data held by the estate agent. The estate agent accepts the need for rectification and changes the Personal Data that they hold. They must also inform the mortgage broker and encourage them to make the same changes.

## Right to Erasure

Under Article 17 of the GDPR individuals have the right to have personal data erased. This is also known as the 'right to be forgotten'. The right is not absolute and only applies in certain circumstances. The most important of these are:

- the purpose the Personal Data was originally being processed for no longer requires that data;

- the Personal Data was being processed on the basis of consent and this has been withdrawn by the Data Subject;
- the Personal Data was being processed on the basis of legitimate interests, the Data Subject has objected to that processing and there is no overriding legitimate interest which would justify ignoring that objection;
- the Personal Data was being processed for direct marketing purposes and the individual objects to that processing;
- that the Personal Data was being processed unlawfully without a lawful basis for processing; and
- there is a legal obligation to delete the data.

One of the most difficult areas for many people to understand is the issue of electronic backups. Backups of electronic data are good practice and are, in fact, required by the GDPR as it is concerned not just with restricting the processing of Personal Data but also the protection of the integrity of that data. As a result, an effective backup strategy is a core part of GDPR compliance. However, the very existence of an effective backup strategy means that an erasure request is either very expensive to fulfil as it will require all existing backups to be replaced, or doomed to failure as the backup will always contain some of that data. However, this issue has been considered. Recital 67 makes clear that the main purpose of erasure is not so much to remove the Personal Data from existence but to place it beyond use so that it cannot be processed or changed and is not readily available to users. In other words, it is not necessary to start going through every backup to delete Personal Data as a result of an erasure request provided that this data is not going to be used and provided that there is a proper backup structure in place which allows for reasonable turnover of backup data.

For example, a law firm has a backup strategy in place in which they take a full backup of their data every month at the end of the month, a differential backup each week on a Sunday which shows the changes since the last full backup, and then a daily differential backup which shows the changes between the last weekly backup. Therefore to recover all the data on a Tuesday in the second week of the month there will be a need to use the last full monthly backup taken at the end of January, the weekly differential taken at the end of week one, and the daily differential backup taken at the end of Monday. In addition, the firm retains the previous month's backups in case there is a need to roll data back. In the event of an erasure request the daily differential backup would show that the data was to be put beyond use. The data erasure would roll through the backup sequence and two months after the erasure request the data would be entirely gone once the backup month was deleted. This is likely to be acceptable in most cases unless the data was especially sensitive as it is the view of the ICO that where an erasure request is made that as long as the backup strategy is effective in removing data completely within a reasonable period then it is likely to be acceptable. However, the ICO is also of the view that the timeline for total deletion must be communicated to the person seeking to have their data erased.

Where a Data Controller has passed data to a third party, whether it is a Data Processor working for the Data Controller or some other organisation then the Data Controller must take steps to have that data erased. Where the data has been publicised, for example being placed on a public website and then indexed by a search engine, recital 66 also states that a Data Controller is required to seek to have that further indexing removed as well. This would involve contacting major search engines such as Google or Bing to ask them to erase their cache of the data and remove the links. The CJEU held in 2014[21] that individuals could request delisting from a search engine and the EDPB is clear in its guidelines on search engines that this was part of the basis for the right to erasure in the GDPR. The UK High Court has also held that in the context of rehabilitation of offenders the right to erasure of links to news stories about offending had to be balanced against the competing rights to freedom of expression and freedom of information.[22] That would be a fine balance and the general benefit to society of the information continuing to be available would be a key element in the decision.

Erasure rights do not apply where there is a requirement to comply with a legal obligation or for the establishment, exercise or defence of legal claims. So a law firm could refuse to delete its files if those files are being maintained to allow the firm and its clients to later protect themselves from legal claims or to allow them to make such claims. So, if a former client has intimated that they intend to make a claim against a law firm and then demands deletion of their files as they contain Personal Data then the law firm could legitimately refuse on the basis that the data was required in order to be able to defend a legal claim.

## Restriction of Processing

A Data Subject is permitted by Article 18 to ask for processing to be restricted in the sense of seeking to limit the manner in which a Data Controller is using their Personal Data. This is intended as an alternative to seeking to have the data erased altogether.

As the GDPR requires organisations to limit processing as far as

---

[21] In *Google Spain SL and Google Inc. v Agencia Española de Protección de Datos (AEPD) and Mario Costeja González*, Case C-131/12.

[22] *NT 1 & NT 2 v Google LLC* [2018] EWHC 799 (QB).

possible and not process Personal Data when they have no need to do so the concept of restriction is less to do with Data Subjects asking Data Controllers not to process so much of their Personal Data, the Data Controller should be doing that already! Instead restriction is intended as an interim measure to allow something else to occur. This is made clear by the four scenarios in which a processing restriction can be sought. These are:

1. The Data Subject is questioning the accuracy of their Personal Data island the Data Controller is verifying the accuracy;

2. The Personal Data is being processed outside the limits of the GDPR but instead of having it deleted the Data Subject requests that the Personal Data is processed in a more limited manner;

3. The Data Controller no longer needs to process the Personal Data but it is needed by the Data Subject to establish, exercise or defence of legal claims;

4. The Data Subject has objected to data processing pursuant and the Data Controller is considering their response.

So for example, a law firm may have decided that they will destroy their conveyancing file on a property transaction and delete all records in accordance with their normal process for doing so. The former client could make a restriction request seeking that they do not delete the file as they anticipate needing the information in the papers to deal with a boundary dispute with their neighbour.

Recital 67 suggests that a Data Controller could practically restrict processing by moving data to another system, making it unavailable to users, or removing it from publication. For most processing systems making data unavailable is probably the easiest option but it will require the system to be designed to allow this. This is a perfect example of the need to have data protection concepts built into system design as without them it is hard to practically restrict processing.

If Personal Data is being restricted the Data Controller must inform everyone they have given that data to so that they can also restrict processing of the same Personal Data. If the Data Controller decides that they will lift the restriction, which is mainly where they have come to a decision on accuracy or objection they must inform the Data Subject before the restriction is lifted.

As with other rights identity information can be sought if it is reasonably necessary to do so but cannot be sought as a matter of course. Again, as with other rights restriction can be refused on the basis it is unfounded or excessive. So, for example, an individual has asked a law firm to delete and rectify data on several occasions and has been refused every time. They then make a request for restriction of processing. This is likely to be an unfounded request.

A restriction request must be complied with without undue delay and in any event within one calendar month. The exact time will depend on the complexity of the request and the importance to the Data Subject. So a request to restrict processing by not deleting Personal Data is likely to need a rapid response as if it is not dealt with quickly the data will be deleted and this is likely to cause significant detriment to the Data Subject.

### Right to Object

Article 21 of the GDPR gives Data Subjects the right to object to data processing in certain circumstances. The two most relevant circumstances which allow for an objection are where Personal Data is being used for direct marketing and where the Data Controller is relying on legitimate interests as a processing basis.

Where an objection is to direct marketing activity this is an absolute right and there is no basis for refusal.

So, for example, an estate agent has decided to send a direct mailshot to every house owner on a street where they have previously sold a property. They have obtained the names and addresses of every owner from the Land Registry for this purpose. One of the householder's objects to this processing. The estate agent must comply and cease processing the Personal Data for this purpose.

Where the Data Controller is relying on a legitimate interest to process the Personal Data then if there is an objection made then the Data Controller must consider this and establish that their own legitimate interest in the data processing activity overrides that of the Data Subject. The carrying out of an impact assessment for the legitimate interests processing is very useful in making this decision.

So, for example, a law firm that is using legitimate interests as the basis to contact former clients with details of ancillary services that will potentially be of interest to them receives an objection to this processing activity from an individual. They are unlikely to be able to show that their marketing activity is an interest that overrides the right to object. Therefore the firm will need to stop marketing to that individual. However, this does not prevent the overall marketing continuing to other clients who have not objected.

Again as with other right identity information can be sought where it is reasonably needed and objections can be refused if they are unfounded or excessive.

## Right to Portability

Data Subjects also have a right under Article 20 to have access to their personal data which is stored by a Data Controller and to have that data sent to another Data Controller directly. It is important to bear in mind that this right is limited to a Data Subject's own Personal Data that they have provided to the Data Controller directly or through their own actions and not necessarily all data that a Data Controller is in possession of. In particular, this is unlikely to apply to any material that the Data Controller has generated from the data they were provided. So, what in the United States is commonly referred to as "work product", that is work that a solicitor generates based on the material their client has provided is not likely to be covered. For example, a client has engaged a solicitor in a piece of litigation. They disagree over the best manner to progress the case and the client seeks to exercise his right to data portability. The solicitor is seeking to exercise a lien over some of the papers so that he can have his bills settled. The right to portability would apply to the information originally provided by the client by email to the solicitor but it would not apply to the draft particulars of claim produced by the solicitor from that information.

Where Personal Data includes that of a third party then a balance must be struck between their rights and that of the Data Subject. However, as data portability principally applies to data provided to the Data Controller by the Data Subject in the first place there should be little need to provide third party data that the Data Subject did not in fact have already.

The key point about data portability is the means of provision. When a Data Controller provides data in this way it is required to be in a structured electronic format which is in common use. The idea being that a Data Subject can take their business away from a Data Controller and easily move to a new Data Controller without a need to provide all the basis details to the new Data Controller from scratch.

In effect, this is an effort to create a system similar to that which price comparison sites have done for the consumer insurance market by permitting a single input of data to be used by multiple firms to the benefit of the individual.

## Rights Relating to Automated Decision Making

Article 22 of the GDPR prevents Data Controllers from making decisions entirely by automated means where those decisions will have a significant effect on an individual or alter their legal rights. This means that there is no human involvement in the decision-making process at all.

So, a letting agent that asked tenants to fill in an online form which they then ran through an entirely automated credit scoring system and provided an automated acceptance or rejection would not be permitted. If however, the online form was used to obtain a credit score which an employee of the agency then reviewed and came to a decision about the application then this would be permissible.

Automated decision making is allowed where it is:

- necessary for entering into or perform of a contract between the Data Controller or another organisations and Data Subject;
- Specifically authorised by law; or
- The Data Subject has explicitly consented to this.

So a letting agent that was using an entirely automated system to carry out a right to rent check would be likely to be permitted to do this as it is a necessity for the commencement of a tenancy agreement.

## Exemptions to the Rights

There are some specific exemptions to the various rights given to Data Subjects. These are authorised but the GDPR but set out (within the boundaries permitted by the GDPR) by the UK government and can be found in the Schedules to the DPA 18. There are a wide range of exemptions so I will focus here on the ones that are most likely to be relevant:

- **Crime** – There are some fairly wide exemptions around the prevention and detection of crime. In particular there are fairly wide exemptions from the GDPR principles and most Data Subject rights as well. However, this is only to the extent that these rights would prevent or undermine the purpose of the processing and potentially enable criminal activity or weaken the response to it. So, for example a conveyancer might decide they need to make a Suspicious Activity Report (SAR) to the National Crime Agency This is exempt from the GDPR and so there is no requirement to inform the client that their Personal Data is being shared in this way and they cannot access the report via an access request.

- **Legal proceedings** – Any disclosure required by law is exempt from the GDPR. This could be a requirement from a statute or regulation or a court order. The exemption also applies to disclosures for legal proceedings, obtaining legal advice, and establishing, exercising, or defending a legal right. So a law firm that was facing a threat of legal action for negligence from a client would be able to disclose their file to the law firm nominated by their professional indemnity insurer to obtain legal advice. The client could not prevent that disclosure by a demand to restrict processing or a demand for erasure of the file.

- **Legal Professional Privilege** – The right to privilege is also exempted from the GDPR. it is important to remember that not everything done by a law firm is privileged but any aspect of legal advice is likely to be. So, to use the example above, a client who had threatened a law firm with legal proceedings for negligence cannot use an access request to see a copy of legal advice obtained by that law firm from the solicitor nominated by their professional indemnity insurer. Likewise a Data Subject who demands erasure or objects to processing by an estate agent could not then demand to see legal advice obtained from a data protection solicitor about the extent of that estate agent's rights and obligations. However, notably, because of the very tight boundaries around privilege advice obtained from a non-lawyer data protection specialist might well be disclosable.

- **Self incrimination** – Schedule 2, paragraph 19 of the DPA 18 also allows for the GDPR provisions relating to the right to be informed and the right to access to be ignored where complying with them would provide evidence that an organisation had committed an offence. However, there is a key limit on this as the exemption does not apply where the offence is one under the DPA 18 itself. So it is not open to an organisation to breach the DPA 18 and the GDPR and then use the fact of that offending to then conceal the breach.

- **Public protection** – there are a group of exemptions which relate to the protection of the public. The most relevant is the one relating to worker safety. This provides exemptions to GDPR rights to the extent that complying with them would prejudice activity intended to secure the health, safety, or welfare of workers. However, if you can comply with the GDPR without prejudicing safety then you must do so. So, a factory that operated a whistle-blower policy around internal office safety would be entitled not to provide copies of records of reports made under that policy.

- **Legal service complaint handling** – Complaints about legal services are exempt under Schedule 2, paragraph 10 of DPA 18. This exempts all aspects of considering a complaint made under the Legal Services Act 2007. So a law firm that is the subject of a client complaint cannot have its internal considerations accessed by that client under the GDPR.

- **Management forecasting and planning** – management planning is exempt from disclosure under the right of access. So an estate agent that is making plans to carry out a redundancy exercise cannot be forced to disclose that planning if an individual makes an access request before the redundancy exercise was announced to staff.

These are not the only exemptions but they are the ones most relevant to organisations in the property sector. In general, the GDPR is not intended to allow people to circumvent other common law or legislative provisions relating to confidentiality and business practices that reasonably need to be confidential for the overall health of the business and these exemptions are designed to support that. However, none of them are blanket exemptions and Personal Data must be handled within the GDPR to the fullest extent possible taking these limits into account.

# CHAPTER SIX
# REGULATION

## Supervisors

The GDPR is a pan-European exercise, spanning multiple jurisdictions. Each of them has one or more data protection supervisors. In the UK this is the Information Commissioner's Office or ICO. The specific data protection supervisor which has oversight of any particular Data Controller or Data Processor is the one which covers the jurisdiction in which they are established, not the one which covers the location where the data actually resides or is dealt with. Therefore most people reading this text will be subject to the oversight of the ICO, notwithstanding that the Personal Data they are handling might be elsewhere. In fact, the Personal Data will almost certainly will be elsewhere as many cloud data centres in the EEA are in the Irish Republic.

This has led to some criticism of the GDPR in practice. This is because the actual burden of regulation does not fall evenly on each country due to the concentration of computing facilities in specific member states. In addition, few member states have provided their supervisor with the level of support and resources necessary and, particularly, with sufficient technical resources to perform their regulatory function effectively. Therefore the GDPR is not entirely fulfilling its objective due to a lack of effective enforcement activity.

## Data Protection Fees

The GDPR itself does not require a fee to be paid to a supervisory body. However, the ICO is able to charge a fee under the Digital Economy Act 2017. The fee structure is set by the Data Protection

(Charges and Information) Regulations 2018. These were amended by the Data Protection (Charges and Information) (Amendment) Regulations 2019 but this change only exempted Peers, MPs, and prospective MPs from data protection fees. The fee is in three tiers of £40, £60, and £2,900. The exact fee payable depends on the business annual turnover and number of staff. Charities always fall into the lower tier regardless of size and in principle all Data Controller and Data Processors are liable to pay. There are exemptions to the fee payment where the only Personal Data being processed is that of employees and clients and relates to activities involved in keeping accounts and sales records, marketing and advertising to clients, and the making of financial forecasts in relation to the organisation's own business.

## Data Breaches

The GDPR in Article 33 creates an important new duty on a Data Controller to notify the relevant supervisory authority where there has been a breach of the GDPR leading to a risk to Personal Data. Data Processors do not have to notify a supervisory authority but Article 33(2) require them to notify the Data Controller without "undue delay". The Data Controller would then be obliged to notify the supervisory authority. Contrary to what many believe a data breach involves rather more than communicating data to the wrong person. It also includes situations where Personal Data is altered without proper approval or is rendered unavailable by loss, deletion (even on a temporary basis until restored from a backup), or a malware attack. However, one of the most common data breaches is the more simple accidental sending of an email to the wrong recipient.

Not every breach is reportable. The ICO only requires breaches that result in a real risk to the rights and freedoms of a Data Subject to be reported. If the breach is likely to result in a risk then it must be reported. If the risk is negligible then a report is not necessary. The

Art 29 WP has stated that when assessing risk consideration the type of data breach, the sensitivity and volume of data lost, the ease of identification of Data Subjects from that lost data, and how serious the consequences for them are should all be considered.

For example, a law firm stores original wills it has prepared for clients. It does not keep any copies or backups. A fire causes the destruction of a small cabinet containing 20 such wills. The Personal Data in these wills has not been disclosed but it has been destroyed. The Personal Data cannot be easily recovered and so there is a significant risk to the rights of Data Subjects as the Personal Data is sensitive and the consequences of its loss are serious. This is likely to be reportable to the ICO.

In another example, during a conveyancing transaction a draft Land Registry transfer document which was meant to be emailed to the client is accidentally sent to an admitted fee earner in another law firm which it entirely unconnected with the transaction. She is contacted immediately by telephone and asked to delete the email without reading it. She confirms that she has done so. The Data Subject's Personal Data has been disclosed inappropriately but the person it has been disclosed to is trustworthy and has deleted the data so the risk to the Data Subject is low. This is unlikely to be reportable to the ICO.

Just because a breach is not reportable does not mean it should be ignored. Internally, all breaches should be reported and then the appropriate person should make a decision on whether or not to report that breach to the ICO. A note should be kept of the facts of the breach, its effects, the remediation actions taken to stop it happening again, and the reasoning for the decision to report or otherwise-especially if the decision is not to report.

A breach report must include:

- A description of the breach including any categories of Data

Subject involved (eg. customers, employees etc.) and an estimate of the number of people affected as well as the type of data involved and the number of records involved;

- The contact details of the data protection officer or other organisational contact;

- A description of the expected consequences of the breach; and

- Any steps taken or planned to deal with the breach. This would also include steps intended to reduce the effect of the breach where possible.

Where a breach is reportable it must be reported within 72 hours of the Data Controller becoming aware of it at the latest and ideally far sooner. If the report is later than 72 hours from discovery it must be accompanied by an explanation for that delay. It is worth noting that the ICO has been very clear that it expects reports to be made well within 72 hours. The GDPR does not require all the details to be in a single breach report and it can be done in phases and so the ICO expects reports to be made inside the window even if all the necessary data is not yet available. The Art 29 WP has stated that awareness means when a Data Controller has a reasonable degree of certainty that a breach has occurred. So, this will not be immediately the problem is discovered but as soon as it is broadly established that a loss has occurred. So, a Data Controller may initially suspect that their systems have been hacked but it may take an hour to confirm that and a further hour to establish that it is likely that Personal Data was accessed. That would be the point at which they became aware and the 72-hour clock began to run. Conversely if a USB stick with unencrypted Personal Data is lost it will not be possible for a Data Controller to know if or when it has been accessed but there is a substantial risk that will happen. So, the point of awareness comes as soon as the loss is discovered.

For example, a law firm suffers a malware attack which encrypts a large number of client records and also damages the shorter-term backups. However, it is not initially clear whether data can be recovered from older backups. A report should be made to the ICO with an initial estimate of the number of clients and records affected but with a note stating that this is likely to be reduced as older backups are used to recover some data. Once the final losses are known the report should be updated.

Where a data breach has the potential to result in a high risk to the rights of an individual then Article 34 requires it to be reported to the individual concerned as well as to the ICO. The report to the individual should contain similar information to that provided to the ICO but with a greater emphasis on any mitigation measures that individuals can take to protect themselves. Ideally this should be done by direct communication unless the cost and effort are out of proportion to the risk. If direct communication is not possible then a public notification should be made, for example by a notice on the organisation's website.

Individual notification is only required in cases of high risk to individual rights, that is a higher threshold than a report to the ICO. The key point to take into account when considering a report to an individual is that the main purpose of such a report is to allow the individual to take steps to reduce their risk. So if there is some practical step that individuals could take which would reduce their risk then a notification would be sensible. For example, if an organisation suffers a data breach leading to a loss of credit card numbers then this puts Data Subjects at a substantial risk of financial loss. Notification would allow them to cancel cards and protect themselves from this risk.

The speed of notification to individuals is not specified. The requirement is only to do so without undue delay. Recital 86 also encourages these communications to be made in cooperation with the relevant supervisory authority. So an early report to the relevant supervisor accompanied by a request fro guidance on notification to individuals would normally be an appropriate way to proceed. At the same time recital 88 says that a report should avoid prejudicing the investigations of law enforcers wherever possible. Therefore in some cases it may be necessary to consult with the Police to discuss how a report should be made and what it should contain to avoid prejudicing an investigation.

In some cases informing individuals may not be required. Article 34(3) states that communication is not required where the data is subject to appropriate technical measures which make it useless to anyone in possession of it. So if Personal Data is encrypted and only the encrypted material is lost then a report to individuals is not required although it may still be necessary to make a report to the ICO.

The ICO has a very useful self-assessment tool to help consider whether a breach report should be made. It also provides a reporting template for recording and reporting data breaches.[23] It is recommended that the template is used for all internal data breach reporting as it is independent of the ICO and does not force a report to be made. However, the report will then be recorded internally in a format the ICO will recognise and if a decision is then made to report to the ICO the report will already be in the correct format with the appropriate questions answered.

## Documents and Records

Article 30 requires Data Controllers and Data Processors to maintain records of data processing activities. The required information is mainly the same as is required by a privacy notice. So organisations must record:

---

[23] See https://ico.org.uk/for-organisations/report-a-breach/personal-data-breach/

- The details of their organisation and (where applicable) the DPO- this will normally be recorded anyway;

- The purpose or purposes of the various data processing activities being carried out;

- The categories of Data Subjects and Personal Data which is being processed;

- The recipients of any Personal Data;

- Details of any Personal Data transfers to third countries outside the EEA;

- Schedules showing the retention and deletion of Personal Data; and

- A description of the security measures for Personal Data that are in place, whether technical or operational in nature.

In addition the ICO advises recording activities undertaken to be in compliance with the GDPR and DPA 18. This is not explicitly required under the GDPR but doing so would be required under the accountability principle. This would require recording such things as:

- Staff training records;

- Records of consents;

- Data Controller/Data Processor contracts;

- Data Protection Impact Assessments;

- Records of Personal Data breaches.

## Codes and Certifications

The GDPR intentionally has much greater allowance for code of conduct and certifications than the former regime. In particular, it allows trade and professional bodies to create codes and certification schemes that can be approved by national supervisory authorities or even at a pan-EEA level. Codes and certifications are intended to fill the gaps in the GDPR in practice by distilling its general statements of outcomes that must be achieved into a more detailed set of rules that must be followed which are attuned to a specific sector.

A code of conduct is aimed at small and medium enterprises while certifications are available for all business sizes. However, those are not exclusive criteria and there is no reason why a large business could not make use of a Code of Conduct. The real difference between a code and a certification is what it covers. A code can be quite specific and cover just one part of the GDPR. So article 40 gives examples of codes covering discrete such as "the legitimate interest pursued by controllers in specific contexts". By contrast a certification is more all-embracing and needs to cover the full sweep of the GDPR.

From the perspective of a Data Controller the advantage of a code or certification is that it can simplify part or all of the process of GDPR compliance by giving a much clearer set of rules and standards to follow. In addition, a Data Controller who is in compliance with an accreditation regime or a code of practice will be assumed to be meeting the accountability principle to the extent that the code or accreditation scheme covers. The ICO has also indicated that it is more likely to see an organisation that adheres to a code or certification as seeking to meet its obligations and while that does not mean that they will be lenient it does mean that they are likely to give the benefit of any doubt to such an organisation. So, as an example the Law

Society could develop its Lexcel legal practice quality mark standard such that it included an approved code of practice and firms that signed up to this code would be assumed to meet the GDPR accountability principle to the extent of the code unless the contrary was shown.

Currently, there are no approved codes or certifications. There was a substantial delay initially as the ICO was not prepared to approve anything or even discuss approval until the EDPB had gone through a consultation process and finalised its own guidance on codes and certifications. As the UK has now left the EU the ICO is no longer bound by the EDPB and so the EDPB and ICO have both issued their own guides on codes and certifications. At the current time no codes or certifications have been approved at the EU level. While the ICO has also yet to approve any codes it has stolen something of a march on the EDPB by approving three certification schemes for the GDPR. These relate to the deletion of personal data during the destruction and disposal of IT equipment and age assurance and the handling of children's personal data.[24] The initial approval of three certification schemes by the ICO is likely to lead to further interest in GDPR codes and certifications.

## Enforcement and Penalties

The GDPR substantially increases the power of supervisory bodies and, in particular massively increases fining powers available to supervisory bodies. For a less severe breach of the GDPR the maximum fine is in principle now  10 million (about £9 million) or 2% of the organisation's worldwide turnover from the previous financial year. For a more serious breach the maximum fine if  20 million (about £18 million) or 4% of the previous financial year's

[24] See https://ico.org.uk/about-the-ico/news-and-events/news-and-blogs/2021/08/ico-approves-the-first-uk-gdpr-certification-scheme-criteria/

turnover. This potentially allows for massive fines for breaches.

The ICO has continually emphasised its desire to be a light touch regulator. In truth, it has little option as, in common with most other European data protection supervisors, it is severely under-resourced and has insufficient staff with expertise in information technology to perform its role effectively. That said, it is not to be ignored and while it is under-resourced that does not mean it does not act where it can.

The ICO has a range of powers it can exercise to investigate compliance with the GDPR and deal with a failure to comply. These include:

- conducting assessments for GDPR compliance either on notice or without any notice in extreme cases;

- issuing an information notice requiring information to be provided to the ICO. Again these can be on little notice and can be enforced by court order;

- reviewing organisation's data protection impact assessments;

- ordering an organisation to inform an individuals about a data breach;

- issuing a warning where the ICO considers that a planned course of action may not comply with the GDPR or reprimands where it has already been breached;

- issuing enforcement notices requiring actions to remedy GDPR breaches or to prevent breaches occurring.

- issuing penalty notices for GDPR breaches;

- prosecuting offences.

The ICO can also take a range of actions that fall short of formal actions including providing letters of advice and various forms of face-to-face advice and guidance sessions.

The ICO has consulted on a guide to its penalty structure. In general this operates at a far lower level than was previously expected when the GDPR was first put forward.

As an example the ICO initially was expected to fine British Airways a sum in excess of £180 million for the widely publicised data breach in which it lost data of over 400,000 customers. Following its draft policy that fine was reduced to just £20 million. By contrast other countries within the EEA appear to be issuing far greater fines and even increasing them. The Irish DPC recently fined WhatsApp 225 million. The original fine proposed by the DPC was actually £50 million but under a process operated by the EDPB the Irish decision was objected to by a number of other data protection supervisory bodies and the DPC was forced to increase it substantially.[25]

The ICO's penalty consultation has three levels of fixed penalty for micro, small to medium and large organisations for technical offences such as failure to register with the ICO. These fixed penalties are relatively low at £400, £600, and £4,000 respectively. For more serious offences the ICO will decide on seriousness and culpability and will use these to establish a starting point based on percentage of worldwide turnover. These percentages are comparatively small in most cases. Even in a case where an organisation is negligent and the seriousness is rated at the highest level the maximum startng point is set at 2% of turnover. It is only for wilful breaches of the GDPR that the ICO proposes to impose the very highest levels of penalty. While

---

[25] See https://edpb.europa.eu/news/news/2021/edpb-requests-irish-sa-amends-whatsapp-decision-clarifications-transparency-and_en

the ICO has yet to formally have this penalty structure approved it appears that they are already implementing it on an informal basis given the level of fine that is being meted out.

## Private Enforcement

In addition to action by the ICO, individuals can make direct applications to the Court under s167 of the DPA 18 for an order requiring a Data Controller or Data Processor to take or not take specific actions to secure compliance with the GDPR. Under s168 there is also a power to seek compensation for losses or damage caused by a GDPR breach. It has been accepted even under the old data protection regime that damage can include distress so it is not necessary to show that a financial loss has been incurred.[26] The mere fact of the loss of control is sufficient to found a damages claim.[27] However, there must be some genuine distress that arises from a real and tangible threat. So where a law firm sent low level information to the wrong email address and obtained an immediate confirmation that it would be deleted the High Court declined to award damages and in fact awarded costs against the claimants.[28] Cyber-attack is also a difficult area to make a claim under as this does not represent data misuse by the Data Controller but rather a failure to secure that data sufficiently or properly. The High Court has so far declined to impose duties of care in negligence or data misuse in hacking events and so the breach of the statutory duty to secure data properly is currently the only available head of claim. This is a much smaller claim than one which includes a range of negligence and breach of duty claims.[29]

---

26 *Google Inc v Vidal-Hall & Ors* [2015] EWCA Civ 311

27 *Lloyd v Google LLC* [2019] EWCA Civ 1599

28 *Rolfe & Ors v Veale Wasbrough Vizards LLP* [2021] EWHC 2809 (QB)

29 *Warren -v- DGS Retail Limited* [2021] EWHC 2168 (QB)

There has been an explosion in these small-scale claims driven by law firms acting on a conditional fee basis seeking relatively small sums for minor data losses. The legal costs being sought often far outstrip the size of the base claim. In addition, these claims are also often insured which protects the claimant against the risk of defeat in the courts. In contrast to many court claims the insurance premium, called an After the Event (ATE) premium is theoretically recoverable from the defendant directly on the basis that these are media and communication claims. However, they are only media claims if they consist of matters relating to breaches of duty for data misuse, a data protection breach alone is insufficient. Therefore the decision in *Warren* is of particular importance as it renders ATE irrecoverable in most such claims by making them solely about breach of the statutory data protection duty. The further point has been made that these claims are not normally within the jurisdiction of the High Court simply because they are media claims and the sum at issue must justify issuing in the High Court. The removal of the media element of these claims and their limitation to data protection issues will rob them of the necessary value to justify issuing in the High Court.[30]

The Supreme Court has also considered the issue of group claims. There had been an effort to issue a claim against Google on behalf of a large number of unidentified individuals for a relatively small but fixed sum of damages. The Supreme Court rejected this claim structure holding that each such claim would have to be assessed individually.[31] This puts a substantial crimp on the type of mass claims often found in the USA and means that in any such claim there will be a need to identify every potential claimant and for them each to have their claim assessed individually. Given the low value of these claims this is likely to make them much less attractive to law firms and litigation funders looking for a payday.

---

30 *Johnson v Eastlight Community Homes Ltd* [2021] EWHC 3069 (QB)

31 *Lloyd v Google LLC* [2021] UKSC 50

# CHAPTER SEVEN
# CONCLUSION

The GDPR generated a great deal of concern when it first came into force. Many organisations suggested that they would no longer be able to trade as they would lose their ability to market effectively. Those fears were largely based on over-heated misreading of the regulations. What the GDPR has undoubtedly done, however, is massively increased individual awareness of the use of their Personal Data. Complaints to organisations about data use since the GDPR was introduced have continued to increase throughout the UK and EU and the concept of data privacy is deeply ingrained in consumer's minds. The law has consequently developed with some speed and while it is still early days in the life of the GDPR it is clear that it will remain of importance for some time to come. Brexit has not led to the big changes in GDPR that were feared, or hoped for in some quarters and it seems unlikely that massive change will be enacted. The incremental process of divergence between the UK and EU will likely continue but for many organisations the more important and complex problem will be the need to grapple with the large number of international data regimes which have come into effect, partly prompted by the success of the GDPR, and what they mean for their ability to trade abroad.

# GLOSSARY

This glossary serves as a brief definition of commonly used terms in this book and generally in the data protection world.

**Article 29 Working Party**

The Article 29 Working Party is the forerunner to the EDPB and was set up under the old data protection regime that predated the GDPR. Its composition was similar to that which not makes up the EDPB but without a European Data Protection Supervisor as this role was created by the GDPR.

**California Consumer Privacy Act, CCPA**

The CCPA is a recently enacted law in the US state of California which seeks to provide many of the same protections as the GDPR does to Californian residents.

**Data Controller**

A Data Controller is an organisation that is in control of Personal Data and is making use of it either through their own processing or by asking a Data Processor to deal with it on their behalf. Data Controllers are primarily liable for complying with the GDPR.

**Data Processor**

A Data Processor processes Personal Data on the instructions of a Data Controller. They have a more limited set of obligations under the GDPR, largely because they are under the supervision of a Data Controller.

### Data Protection Act 2018

The UK DPA implements the GDPR in the UK. It replaces the old Data Protection Act 1998. Its main function is to set out in detail the various derogations and exemptions which the GDPR permits EEA member states to make use of.

### Data Protection Impact Assessment, DPIA

The Data Protection Impact Assessment or DPIA is a process intended to help assess a data processing operation for compliance with the GDPR and to help minimise the impact of the operation on the rights and freedoms of Data Subjects.

### Data Protection Officer, DPO

A Data Protection Officer is a role created by the GDPR. It is a senior person in an organisation with specific GDPR training who is there to ensure that the GDPR is being complied with. Not all organisations need to have a DPO but where they do have one they must consult with that person.

### Data Protection Supervisor

Each EEA member state has one or more official bodies who are responsible for enforcing the GDPR on organisations that fall within their jurisdiction. In the UK this responsibility falls on the Information Commissioner's Office or ICO. In Eire the responsibility falls on the Data Protection Commission or DPC.

**Data Subject**

A Data Subject is an individual "natural person" whose Personal Data is being processed by a Data Controller or Data Processor.

**European Data Protection Board, EDPB**

The EDPB is the follow on body to the Article 29 Working Party and consists of representatives of data protection supervisors from the various EU nations along with the European Data Protection Supervisor. The EU Commission and the data protection supervisors from the EFTA nations are also involved but have no voting rights. The EDPB is based in Brussels and is independent of the EU.

**General Data Protection Regulation, GDPR**

The GDPR or, to give it its full name, Regulation (EU) 2016/679 of the European Parliament and of the Council of 27 April 2016 on the protection of natural persons with regard to the processing of personal data and on the free movement of such data sets out an entirely new regime for the handling of individuals private information across teh entire EEA and repeals the old regime set out in Directive 95/46/EC of the European Parliament and of the Council of 24 October 1995 on the protection of individuals with regard to the processing of personal data and on the free movement of such data which was implemented in the UK by the Data Protection Act 1998.

**Information Commissioner's Office, ICO**

The ICO is the data protection supervisor for the UK.

**Personal Data**

Personal Data is any data about a Data Subject that is capable of uniquely identifying them.

# MORE BOOKS BY LAW BRIEF PUBLISHING

A selection of our other titles available now:-

| |
|---|
| 'A Practical Guide to Transgender Law' by Robin Moira White & Nicola Newbegin |
| 'Artificial Intelligence – The Practical Legal Issues (2nd Edition)' by John Buyers |
| 'A Practical Guide to Challenging Sham Marriage Allegations in Immigration Law' by Priya Solanki |
| 'A Practical Guide to New Build Conveyancing' by Paul Sams & Rebecca East |
| 'A Practical Guide to Inherited Wealth on Divorce' by Hayley Trim |
| 'A Practical Guide to Shareholder Disputes in Family Businesses' by Ed Weeks |
| 'A Practical Guide to the Law of Forests in Scotland' by Philip Buchan |
| 'A Practical Guide to Health and Medical Cases in Immigration Law' by Rebecca Chapman & Miranda Butler |
| 'A Practical Guide to Bad Character Evidence for Criminal Practitioners by Aparna Rao |
| 'A Practical Guide to Environmental Enforcement' by Christopher Badger & Stuart Jessop |
| 'A Practical Guide to Hoarding and Mental Health for Housing Lawyers' by Rachel Coyle |
| 'A Practical Guide to Psychiatric Claims in Personal Injury – 2nd Edition' by Liam Ryan |
| 'Stephens on Contractual Indemnities' by Richard Stephens |
| 'A Practical Guide to the EU Succession Regulation' by Richard Frimston |
| 'A Practical Guide to Solicitor and Client Costs – 2nd Edition' by Robin Dunne |
| 'Constructive Dismissal – Practice Pointers and Principles' by Benjimin Burgher |
| 'A Practical Guide to Religion and Belief Discrimination Claims in the Workplace' by Kashif Ali |
| 'A Practical Guide to the Law of Medical Treatment Decisions' by Ben Troke |

| |
|---|
| 'Fundamental Dishonesty and QOCS in Personal Injury Proceedings: Law and Practice' by Jake Rowley |
| 'A Practical Guide to the Law in Relation to School Exclusions' by Charlotte Hadfield & Alice de Coverley |
| 'A Practical Guide to Divorce for the Silver Separators' by Karin Walker |
| 'The Right to be Forgotten – The Law and Practical Issues' by Melissa Stock |
| 'A Practical Guide to Planning Law and Rights of Way in National Parks, the Broads and AONBs' by James Maurici QC, James Neill et al |
| 'A Practical Guide to Election Law' by Tom Tabori |
| 'A Practical Guide to the Law in Relation to Surrogacy' by Andrew Powell |
| 'A Practical Guide to Claims Arising from Fatal Accidents – 2nd Edition' by James Patience |
| 'A Practical Guide to the Ownership of Employee Inventions – From Entitlement to Compensation' by James Tumbridge & Ashley Roughton |
| 'A Practical Guide to Asbestos Claims' by Jonathan Owen & Gareth McAloon |
| 'A Practical Guide to Stamp Duty Land Tax in England and Northern Ireland' by Suzanne O'Hara |
| 'A Practical Guide to the Law of Farming Partnerships' by Philip Whitcomb |
| 'Covid-19, Homeworking and the Law – The Essential Guide to Employment and GDPR Issues' by Forbes Solicitors |
| 'Covid-19, Force Majeure and Frustration of Contracts – The Essential Guide' by Keith Markham |
| 'Covid-19 and Criminal Law – The Essential Guide' by Ramya Nagesh |
| 'Covid-19 and Family Law in England and Wales – The Essential Guide' by Safda Mahmood |
| 'A Practical Guide to the Law of Unlawful Eviction and Harassment – 2nd Edition' by Stephanie Lovegrove |
| 'Covid-19, Residential Property, Equity Release and Enfranchisement – The Essential Guide' by Paul Sams and Louise Uphill |
| 'Covid-19, Brexit and the Law of Commercial Leases – The Essential Guide' by Mark Shelton |
| 'A Practical Guide to Costs in Personal Injury Claims – 2nd Edition' by Matthew Hoe |

'A Practical Guide to the General Data Protection Regulation (GDPR) – 2nd Edition' by Keith Markham

'Ellis on Credit Hire – Sixth Edition' by Aidan Ellis & Tim Kevan

'A Practical Guide to Working with Litigants in Person and McKenzie Friends in Family Cases' by Stuart Barlow

'Protecting Unregistered Brands: A Practical Guide to the Law of Passing Off' by Lorna Brazell

'A Practical Guide to Secondary Liability and Joint Enterprise Post-Jogee' by Joanne Cecil & James Mehigan

'A Practical Guide to the Pre-Action RTA Claims Protocol for Personal Injury Lawyers' by Antonia Ford

'A Practical Guide to Neighbour Disputes and the Law' by Alexander Walsh

'A Practical Guide to Forfeiture of Leases' by Mark Shelton

'A Practical Guide to Coercive Control for Legal Practitioners and Victims' by Rachel Horman

'A Practical Guide to Rights Over Airspace and Subsoil' by Daniel Gatty

'Tackling Disclosure in the Criminal Courts – A Practitioner's Guide' by Narita Bahra QC & Don Ramble

'A Practical Guide to the Law of Driverless Cars – Second Edition' by Alex Glassbrook, Emma Northey & Scarlett Milligan

'A Practical Guide to TOLATA Claims' by Greg Williams

'A Practical Guide to Elderly Law – 2nd Edition' by Justin Patten

'A Practical Guide to the Law of Prescription in Scotland' by Andrew Foyle

'A Practical Guide to the Construction and Rectification of Wills and Trust Instruments' by Edward Hewitt

'A Practical Guide to the Law of Bullying and Harassment in the Workplace' by Philip Hyland

'How to Be a Freelance Solicitor: A Practical Guide to the SRA-Regulated Freelance Solicitor Model' by Paul Bennett

'A Practical Guide to Prison Injury Claims' by Malcolm Johnson

'A Practical Guide to the Small Claims Track - 2nd Edition' by Dominic Bright

'A Practical Guide to Advising Clients at the Police Station' by Colin Stephen McKeown-Beaumont

'A Practical Guide to Antisocial Behaviour Injunctions' by Iain Wightwick

'Practical Mediation: A Guide for Mediators, Advocates, Advisers, Lawyers, and Students in Civil, Commercial, Business, Property, Workplace, and Employment Cases' by Jonathan Dingle with John Sephton

'The Mini-Pupillage Workbook' by David Boyle

'A Practical Guide to Crofting Law' by Brian Inkster

'A Practical Guide to Spousal Maintenance' by Liz Cowell

'A Practical Guide to the Law of Domain Names and Cybersquatting' by Andrew Clemson

'A Practical Guide to the Law of Gender Pay Gap Reporting' by Harini Iyengar

'A Practical Guide to the Rights of Grandparents in Children Proceedings' by Stuart Barlow

'NHS Whistleblowing and the Law' by Joseph England

'Employment Law and the Gig Economy' by Nigel Mackay & Annie Powell

'A Practical Guide to Noise Induced Hearing Loss (NIHL) Claims' by Andrew Mckie, Ian Skeate, Gareth McAloon

'An Introduction to Beauty Negligence Claims – A Practical Guide for the Personal Injury Practitioner' by Greg Almond

'Intercompany Agreements for Transfer Pricing Compliance' by Paul Sutton

'Zen and the Art of Mediation' by Martin Plowman

'A Practical Guide to the SRA Principles, Individual and Law Firm Codes of Conduct 2019 – What Every Law Firm Needs to Know' by Paul Bennett

'A Practical Guide to Adoption for Family Lawyers' by Graham Pegg

'A Practical Guide to Industrial Disease Claims' by Andrew Mckie & Ian Skeate

'A Practical Guide to Redundancy' by Philip Hyland

'A Practical Guide to Vicarious Liability' by Mariel Irvine

'A Practical Guide to Applications for Landlord's Consent and Variation of Leases' by Mark Shelton

'A Practical Guide to Relief from Sanctions Post-Mitchell and Denton' by Peter Causton

'A Practical Guide to Equity Release for Advisors' by Paul Sams

'A Practical Guide to Financial Services Claims' by Chris Hegarty

www.ingramcontent.com/pod-product-compliance
Lightning Source LLC
LaVergne TN
LVHW022102200926
848481LV00003B/1043
* 9 7 8 1 9 1 4 6 0 8 3 3 9 *